How to Beat

Depression

One Step at a Time

How to Beat
Depression

One Step at a Time

**Marie Chellingsworth
and Paul Farrand**

ROBINSON

ROBINSON

First published in Great Britain in 2015 by Robinson

Copyright © Marie Chellingsworth and Paul Farrand, 2015

3 5 7 9 10 8 6 4 2

The moral right of the authors has been asserted.

Important Note
This book is not intended as a substitute for medical advice
or treatment. Any person with a condition requiring medical
attention should consult a qualified medical practitioner or
suitable therapist.

A CIP catalogue record for this book
is available from the British Library.

ISBN 978-1-47210-883-8

Typeset in Minion by Initial Typesetting Services, Edinburgh
Printed and bound in Great Britain by Clays Ltd, St Ives plc

Papers used by Robinson are from well-managed forests
and other responsible sources

MIX
Paper from
responsible sources
FSC® C104740

Robinson
An imprint of
Little, Brown Book Group
Carmelite House
50 Victoria Embankment
London EC4Y 0DZ

An Hachette UK Company
www.hachette.co.uk

www.littlebrown.co.uk

CONTENTS

CONTENTS

GETTING GOING

Great start!

Sometimes the hardest steps are the first ones. Just by picking this self-help book up and beginning to read it you have taken a big step forwards. It is often very difficult to get going. So it is great that you have taken this first step!

The techniques in this book have helped many people feel better. An important part of feeling better is getting back to doing the things you want to be able to do. We hope the techniques will benefit you to do just that. This self-help book will form your own personal toolkit. Working through it will provide you with a range of ways to understand and feel more in control of your mood.

Things can feel overwhelming when your mood is low. So we have written the book in short sections and you can work through it at a pace that suits you. We have also included examples of other people who have used the techniques when they felt low.

These show how they put the techniques into action in their daily life to improve how they were feeling. They have also provided us with some top tips to share with you about using this toolkit.

They are honest accounts that show there are things you can do that will help. It is not always easy, and there is no quick fix. But by breaking things down, and doing them step by step, small changes lead to bigger change.

Getting to know us

First of all we would like to introduce ourselves. We want tell you a little about who we are and why we have written this book. We both work at the University of Exeter, running courses in Cognitive Behavioural Therapy (CBT). We also work clinically with patients. CBT is an evidence-based treatment. It is recommended for people with low mood, depression and anxiety and is the approach used in this book. We have taught many other practitioners to use CBT to help other people. We have both worked with the Department of Health and other organisations to help set standards for training and delivery of CBT in England.

Marie Chellingsworth: I am a senior lecturer and course director. I lead training programmes for

Psychological Wellbeing Practitioners (PWPs) and undergraduate Applied Psychiatry (Clinical) students. I am passionate about CBT training and ensuring people over the age of 65 get equal access to treatment. Clinically my interest areas are working with adults with depression and anxiety disorders. Much of this work is with carers, particularly those caring for people who need palliative care or who have dementia. I am renovating an old 1800s lodge in Devon that I share with my Irish setter Alfie and cat Hendrix. Outside of work I love good music and spending time with friends. (My secret pleasure is watching *Emmerdale*!)

Paul Farrand: I am a senior lecturer and health psychologist. Clinically most of my work has been with people with physical health problems and depression. Most recently I worked with people in hospital with head, neck and jaw problems. My current research focus is developing CBT self-help for people with dementia and armed forces veterans. Outside of work I enjoy spending time with my wife, Paula, and our three children, Oliver, Ellis and Amélie. We enjoy eating out and long walks in the East Devon countryside and coastline with our two black Labradors. I also have an interest in 1950s British cinema.

So what is cognitive behavioural therapy?

This book is based on an evidence-based treatment called cognitive behavioural therapy, or CBT for short. CBT is the treatment for people with depression and anxiety recommended by the National Institute of Health and Care Excellence (NICE). This recommendation is based on many research trials that show CBT is effective for lots of people with depression and anxiety. We can personally recommend CBT based on our own clinical practice. We will explain more about CBT and how it works later in this section.

Using self-help

This book uses a self-help approach. It gives you the tools that you can put into practice at a pace that suits you. You may have used some kind of self-help before, or this may be your first time using self-help. If you are struggling with your mood, you might initially feel a bit daunted and wonder what lies ahead. That's why we want to start by saying we are here to support you. We have worked hard trying to ensure this book is as easy as possible to read and use. To do this we have taken a lot of advice from people with depression and low mood and followed guidance in writing self-help books.

The important thing to remember is that you don't need to tackle all the book at once. In fact we recommend you don't! One of the advantages of using self-help is that you can use it a time that suits you. You can use it when and where is best for you, this book is always here to help when you want it. You are in charge though. It is what you do that will make the difference for you. To support this we have broken the book down into short sections, to enable you to use it over smaller periods of time if that suits you.

It may be that your healthcare practitioner recommended this self-help book and you will be using it together. If that is the case, they can answer any questions you may have and help you along the way. If not and you are reading this without a healthcare practitioner, you may wish to highlight helpful bits or make notes for yourself as you go along. Other people have told us this is really helpful. Remember if at any time you are not sure about something, you can come back to the book and look at that part again.

How to use this book

We have tried to make using this self-help book as easy as possible for you to use. Some people like to read through things first and then start to use the techniques. Others prefer to start using the techniques straight away. The key thing is to then put the techniques into practice in your daily life. Work through the techniques at a pace that suits you and complete the activities as you go along.

You may want to read about other people who have experienced depression and how this approach helped them. In Section 5 we have included two recovery stories. Here, Bill and Sarah have kindly shared their stories and what they did to feel better. Some people like to read this first, others prefer to read more about CBT and make their own plan first. Either way is fine.

We have broken the book into five sections. You can move through the book in the way that you feel will help you the most.

Section 1: Getting going (page 1)

We begin by looking at depression, its impact and how it can be treated. There are tips for getting started and how to keep going from others with low mood who have used this approach. You can also set goals for where you want to be.

Section 2: Understanding low mood and depression (page 30)

In Section 2 we help you look at how your own mood is affecting you. We introduce the tools that can help, including the CBT technique behavioural activation, and show you how they work

Section 3: Behavioural activation (page 55)

In Section 3 we help you to make your own plan for feeling better by using the CBT technique behavioural activation. You can then put your plan into action and review your progress.

Section 4: The relapse prevention toolkit (page 117)

Section 4 is an important step for when you are feeling better. We help you make a plan for managing your mood in the future and staying well.

Section 5: Recovery stories (page 145)

In Section 5 you can catch up with the people you will first meet in Section 1 in more detail. They have shared their stories of having depression and what helped them. You can see how they put their plans into action and continued to manage their mood.

Top tips before you get going

Before we get started, we would like to share some top tips about using self-help. These tips come from people who have had low mood and depression and from mental health professionals who use CBT.

Top tip 1: Give it your best shot

'I really struggled with getting motivated to begin with. I stuck with it though and I am so glad I did.'

Because you have low mood you may find some things difficult, but give it your best shot. All anyone will ask of you is just that you give things a go. It may help to read the stories of people who have put things into action and now feel better. Later in this section, we ask you to note why you started using this book and the goals you want to achieve. Revisiting these at regular intervals can help to motivate you. If a healthcare practitioner is supporting you, talking to them about times you find things difficult will also help. They can encourage and support you too.

Top tip 2: Put what you learn into action

'What really helped me was doing the things from the book.'

Putting things into action in your daily life is the key way to start feeling better. You may not feel like it at first, but it really works. You don't need to do everything at once. Step-by-step, the book guides you through ways to break things down and get going at a pace that suits you.

Think about using the book to feel better as a bit like how a gym programme helps people get fitter. Just having the gym membership card or a programme doesn't make you fitter or build you instant muscles (if only!). You make yourself fitter by going to the gym and putting the programme into action regularly. It isn't always easy to get going or feel motivated but results come through doing it. The same applies to your mood. This self-help book is here to give you the tools to support you to help you reach your goals. But you will only get the most from it if you then put these tools into action.

Top tip 3: Writing in the book is allowed. In fact we encourage it!

> 'Writing things down was really useful for me as it helped me to take a step back from things. It was also good to be able to look back and see how things were improving in black and white. I couldn't talk myself out of them!'

When we were younger many of us were told that we shouldn't write in books. CBT self-help books are different. They are designed to be written in, in fact the more the better! The more you interact with it and make it personalised for you, the more it can help. To make this easier, each time there is something for you to write we have put in this image.

When you see it, it is a sign for you to write in the book and make a plan. Writing things down can really help you achieve your plan. Also, you will be able to look back in the future and see how far you have come.

Top tip 4: Like everyone, expect to have good days and bad days

'When I started to feel better, I was so pleased and I never wanted to take a step back. Then I had a day where I woke up feeling just like I had done at the start of treatment. I thought my depression had come back and that I would never improve again. I almost gave up. But I stuck with the plan I had in place, and didn't let my mood affect what I did. This meant that I soon got back on track, and the bad feeling didn't last as long. It wasn't easy, as I just wasn't expecting my mood to vary. But now I know my mood does still vary and that is normal. I just carry on and try to not let it affect me.'

Hopefully after using this book for a few weeks you will notice a gradual improvement in your mood. However, you will also have bad days. This may affect how you use your book or engage with the activities. Mood varies for all of us, this is all perfectly normal and to be expected. Just try and keep on track with your plan. Try not to let how you are feeling internally affect what you do.

Top tip 5: Act according to your values, goals and targets, not because of how you feel and think inside

'The most powerful thing that I learned is to act according to my goals, not how I am feeling internally. This helped so much I wrote it on a Post-it Note for my fridge. I also have it as my screen saver on my laptop. This makes me aware of when I am heading into a vicious circle again and helps me to break it.'

A main focus of this book is to act according to your goals and targets, not how you are thinking or feeling internally. You will be asked to set some goals a bit later in this section, and acting according to them is an important way of starting to feel better. Remember, you currently feel like you do because of your low mood. So try not to listen to negative thoughts that are just the depression talking. Do not let it stop you doing things you need to or want to do. We will be exploring this further in Section 2.

Top tip 6: Don't overdo it

'I was initially really pleased with doing the activities I had set as targets. I thought I should get more done while I was feeling like it. I ended up doing lots of things over the course of one weekend and then was exhausted. I couldn't face doing anything I had planned over the next few days. I thought it wasn't working for me and that I had failed. My GP, who was supporting me, helped me to see I was doing too much all at once. I made sure next time I stuck with my targets and didn't overdo it.'

While you can work through the activities at a rate that suits you, slow and steady is what we recommend. We will show you how to break things down into small, manageable chunks. If you are having support from someone while using this book, they can help you with this too. A good tip is to do what you have planned whilst keeping your energy levels at least half full. Sometimes, in the early days, you may find yourself doing less than you may have done before you were depressed. This is OK. The key thing is that you are doing tasks in your daily life and putting your plan into action.

Top tip 7: Involve family and friends if you can

'It really helped me when I discussed my low mood and what I was feeling with my wife. She really wanted to help, and she convinced me to go to the doctor to begin with. I shared this book with her and she

> read it with me. It helped her to under-
> stand what I was struggling with, as well
> as showing her ways she could help me.
> Working together really helped to bring
> us together again. It helped me realise I
> was not alone.'

When you are feeling down, you may have found that having others around can be helpful. They may help you look at things differently, find ways to solve problems or just be there for a chat. However, getting others involved isn't for everyone and you may not be ready to take this step yet. Don't worry if that is the case. But if you think you might find the support of others helpful, and they want to help, then why not ask? They may find the sections in this book on what low mood is and how it is affecting you useful. Why not get them involved and ask them to read this section or discuss it together?

Top tip 8: Set aside time to use the book and set reminders to help you remember

> 'When I started using these techniques, I
> set myself an alert twice a week in the dia-
> ry on my phone. This made sure I set aside
> the time for working through the differ-
> ent sections and activities. It really helped

> **me to not put it off! It was hard to get
> going, but worth it when I got into the
> routine and then began to feel better. It
> is something my GP recommended I did.'**
>
> Many people with depression report prob-
> lems remembering to do things and strug-
> gling to want to do things. Initially these
> difficulties may get in the way of using the
> book to begin with. Setting reminders for
> yourself may help. You can do this whichever
> way is best for you. Many mobile phones now
> have alerts you can set when you are due to
> do something. Other people find putting
> sticky notes on their fridge or cupboard
> doors works just as well.

Getting and using support

At times you may feel like giving up. Don't worry,
it is perfectly normal to occasionally feel that way
or have off-putting thoughts because of your mood.
Those feelings and negative thoughts will pass
and you can keep them in control by still doing
your plan. Keeping going at those times, although
challenging, helps you to keep working towards
feeling better. Using the support of a healthcare

practitioner, a family member or friend that you trust, can also help to keep you motivated and on track.

It may be that you are already receiving support from a GP or other healthcare practitioner. In England, Australia, and spreading to other countries because of their success, are free Improving Access to Psychological Therapies (IAPT) services. They provide support sessions, face-to-face or over the phone, with a psychological wellbeing practitioner (PWP) or coach. These people are specialist mental health practitioners who support you to work through CBT self-help. If you are receiving support it is likely that you will speak to them regularly. They will help you identify and solve any problems and answer any questions you may have.

The focus is on working together, rather than them simply telling you what you should do. There is work for you between sessions to put into practice the techniques and skills that you learn. They will go at the pace you want to go and really put you in control. Remember you are the expert in how you are feeling. Their expertise is in supporting and encouraging your use of this book. Some services also accept self-referral. There can be a waiting time to see someone but they aim to see people as quickly as possible. In England, to find out about

your local IAPT service go to: http://www.iapt.nhs.
uk/services/. Tell whoever is providing the support
that you are using this book, so their support can be
tailored to it.

You may not be receiving support to use this book
or live in an area where IAPT services are available
and may feel that you would benefit from some
support. If this applies you, talk to your GP, who
may have access to other services that can offer support in your local area or who can recommend an
accredited CBT therapist who works in your area.

Equally, you may wish to work through this book
alone or with a friend or family member. That is
also fine. We know that research shows that having
someone to support you to use CBT can make it
more effective. You can access support at any time if
you feel it would be helpful to you. Just contact your
GP or IAPT service if one is available.

We ask two things

There are no rules about how quickly you should
work through the book. There are also no expect-
ations about the amount of time it will take you to
feel better. However, for this to be successful we ask
you to commit to just two things.

1. Give it a go: Read it and do it!

Give the activities a go to see what works for you. The more you can put things into practice, the more likely you will see the benefits. Remember, we all have days when we feel like giving up. Make a commitment to use the book *and* put things into practice. Even if you are not sure it will work for you. Perhaps make a deal with yourself to try it for six weeks and see how you feel.

2. If things get really bad and you think about ending your life, speak to someone straight away

For some people, but not all, when they are depressed things can feel so bad they think about ending their life and may make plans towards this. If things get so bad with your mood that you are having thoughts of ending your life or harming yourself in any way – get help now! There are details of support agencies you can contact 24 hours a day in the further resources at the back of this book (pages 232–233). Let your GP or other health-care practitioner know, they are there to help. Tell someone and get help. Remember you will not always feel this way and that there are things you can do to feel better.

Building motivation to change

As we have said, it can be difficult getting going when you have depression or low mood. Lacking motivation is one of the key symptoms of depression. We have worked with many people who have struggled with motivation and they have found the following activity helpful.

Complete the boxes overleaf to think about what your life will be like again without depression. You can write as much or as little as you like. Then we will help you to set some goals you want to work on.

Building motivation to change: 1

1. Just for a moment visualise what it would be like five years from now if you still had the same feelings you currently have. What would life be like for you? Where would you be going and what would you be doing?

2. Next, visualise what your life will be like in five years from now if you make changes and feel better. Where would you be going? What would you be doing? How would you know you feel better?

> **Building motivation to change:**
> **2 – The miracle question**
>
> Imagine after you go to sleep tonight a miracle happens and when you wake up everything in your life was how you wanted it to be. Write down below what your life would look like if this miracle happened.

Thinking Ahead

Above you have thought about what your life will be like in five years' time without depression. You have also visualised what life could be like when you feel better. Now we would like you to think about getting there and achieving the life you want.

What would you like to achieve over the next few months? Setting some goals can help you to measure your progress and keep you feeling motivated. These may be goals to get back to doing things you have done in the past, or even entirely new things you would like to do. Try and make these goals things that are specific to you, things that you can measure your progress on and that are realistic for you to achieve.

The easiest way to think about a goal is to think what you would be doing if you felt better. Where would you be going? What would life be like? Then try and break these things down into stages. What steps you can take towards the goal you want to achieve in the short, medium and longer term. First come up with two or three bigger goals you would like to achieve from using CBT self-help. Then you can think about things in the short, medium and longer term that you can do towards achieving them. There is an example one filled in below to give you ideas:

My goals for feeling better

Goal 1: ....

Longer term things I can do to work towards this goal over the next six months or so.

_____

_____

_____

Things that I can do towards this goal in the next month.

_____

_____

_____

Things I can do towards this goal in the next couple of weeks.

_____

_____

_____

Goal 2: ....

Longer term things I can do to work towards this goal over the next six months or so.

_____

_____

Things that I can do towards this goal in the next month.

_____

_____

Things I can do towards this goal in the next couple of weeks.

_____

_____

Goal 3: ....

Longer term things I can do to work towards this goal over the next six months or so.

_____

_____

Things that I can do towards this goal in the next month.

_____

_____

Things I can do towards this goal in the next couple of weeks.

_____

_____

Try and make your goals specific to you. Make sure you can measure your progress with them, and that they are realistic for you to achieve.

Now you have your goals, rate each one for how much you are able to do it now, or how much progress you have made towards achieving it. This will be a baseline for you to look back on. By re-rating yourself as you continue through the book, it will allow you to measure how things are improving objectively.

Rating my goals

Goal 1: ....Today's date...................

I can do this now (circle a number):

0	1	2	3	4	5	6
Not at all		Occasionally		Often		Any time

One month re-rating (Today's date...................)
(circle a number):

0	1	2	3	4	5	6
Not at all		Occasionally		Often		Any time

Two month re-rating (Today's date...................)
(circle a number):

0	1	2	3	4	5	6
Not at all		Occasionally		Often		Any time

Three month re-rating (Today's date...................)
(circle a number):

0	1	2	3	4	5	6
Not at all		Occasionally		Often		Any time

Goal 2:.................Today's date...................

I can do this now (circle a number):

0	1	2	3	4	5	6
Not at all		Occasionally		Often		Any time

One month re-rating (Today's date....................)
(circle a number):

0	1	2	3	4	5	6
Not at all		Occasionally		Often		Any time

Two month re-rating (Today's date....................)
(circle a number):

0	1	2	3	4	5	6
Not at all		Occasionally		Often		Any time

Three month re-rating (Today's date.................)
(circle a number):

0	1	2	3	4	5	6
Not at all		Occasionally		Often		Any time

You have now thought about what life will be like
if you make changes and set some goals. We hope
that you feel motivated to continue. Keep going. In
Section 2 we are going to introduce methods that will
help you work towards these goals and feel better.

Goal 3:...............Today's date...................

I can do this now (circle a number):

0	1	2	3	4	5	6
Not at all		Occasionally		Often	Any time	

One month re-rating (Today's date...................)
(circle a number):

0	1	2	3	4	5	6
Not at all		Occasionally		Often	Any time	

Two month re-rating (Today's date...................)
(circle a number):

0	1	2	3	4	5	6
Not at all		Occasionally		Often	Any time	

Three month re-rating (Today's date................)
(circle a number):

0	1	2	3	4	5	6
Not at all		Occasionally		Often	Any time	

You have now thought about what life will be like if you make changes and set some goals. We hope that you feel motivated to continue. Keep going! In Section 2 we are going to introduce the tools that will help you work towards these goals and feel better.

UNDERSTANDING LOW MOOD AND DEPRESSION

People with depression often ask themselves questions like:

What is depression?

Why did it happen to me?

Why does it feel like it's taken over my whole life?

Will it happen again?

What can be done?

In this section we will look at key information about depression and low mood, and answer all the questions above. We will then look at the ways in which your own depression or low mood is affecting you.

The vicious circle of depression

Clinical depression is when feeling down or low continues over a period of weeks, months or even years. Depression covers a range of different symptoms that affect the person's thoughts and physical feelings, and what they do as a result. These three areas – thinking, physical feelings and changes in behaviour – can form a vicious circle and keep us in a spiral of depression.

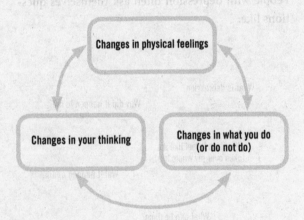

While these are commonly experienced symptoms, depression impacts upon people in different ways. Each person's experience is unique to them. Later in this section you will explore your own vicious circle of the symptoms and changes you are experiencing. This will enable you to think about how each symptom may be keeping your difficulties going.

Real stories of people with depression

We would like to introduce you to two people who have shared their experiences of having depression and using CBT self-help. The techniques covered in this book really helped them feel better. Many people have found reading stories of others who have experienced depression useful and encouraging.

Bill is a 65-year-old painter and decorator who was forced to retire from work. He noticed his mood had become low and that he was giving up lots of things he used to enjoy.

Sarah is a 54 year-old teacher with depression. She had been diagnosed with osteoporosis and her mum had also passed away. A new head teacher had taken over the school she worked in and she started to have problems at work.

The personal situations of Bill and Sarah, their ages or lifestyles, may be different from your own. However, the techniques they have used to help with their depression are the same as the ones that may help you. In Section 5 you can read their full stories and how they used CBT self-help to help them to feel better. They discuss what went well and what they found more challenging, and how they overcame difficulties they found. It may not always be easy for you either, but reading about others' experiences can help to keep you on track.

Bill's story

Bill always intended to continue working after he had reached retirement age. He had worked most of his life as a painter and decorator for a local firm. He had really enjoyed his job and had taken a lot of pride in it. He loved that, through his work, he was always meeting new people. He enjoyed working alongside his colleagues, who he often socialised with outside of work.

When he reached 65, his employer said that for insurance purposes he would not be able to continue working. He was told he had to retire. This devastated Bill, and he soon started to notice his mood becoming lower. He put on a brave face at first. He told his colleagues he was looking forward to being able to fish all day and enjoy his garden. They bought him some lovely gardening tools and new fishing tackle as a leaving present.

After he retired Bill spent most of his days doing very little except sitting around in front of the television. He didn't pay much attention to what was on the TV. Instead he often found himself thinking about how miserable he was feeling. He noticed he felt tired and sluggish most of the time, and he had problems sleeping at night. This made him worry that he might be ill, which was another worrying thought that ran through his mind.

After many arguments with his wife, Pauline, Bill finally agreed to go to his GP and discuss his difficulties. His GP asked him to complete some measures of his mood. They showed Bill was experiencing a moderate to severe level of depression. Bill was shocked at this news and was slightly embarrassed. He thought, 'People like me don't get depressed,' and, 'I should be able to snap out of it.' The

GP told him there were things he could do to help, which Bill found reassuring.

The GP started Bill on a type of anti-depressant called fluoxetine. He also asked him if he wanted to use a self-help book called 'How To Beat Depression One Step at a Time'. He said it would take him through a CBT technique called behavioural activation (which we cover in Section 3).

At first Bill was a little bit sceptical that this could help, but he started to read through the book. He discovered that CBT self-help was widely recommended by the NHS because it really seemed to work. Bill also thought he might like this way of working as it put him in control. It would give him another way to overcome his low mood besides the medication. You can find out how Bill got on with CBT self-help in Section 5 from page 161.

Sarah's story

Sarah was 54 years old and an English teacher. She had worked at the local secondary school for the last 15 years. Her mother had died two years ago, and at the same time a new head teacher had joined the school.

At the age of 53, Sarah had been diagnosed with osteoporosis. She had been having pain in her back that had come on slowly over time. Her consultant had explained that this was due to a compression fracture. He gave her medication and explained that this was a long-term condition. It was important to reduce the risk of future bone breaks.

Sarah wondered what the future held for her. She felt that there was no point in trying to do her hobbies anymore. They would just lead to more pain or increase the risk of her getting a fracture.

As time went on, Sarah found herself questioning her abilities. She was having lots of negative thoughts. 'I am a useless teacher.' 'I can't do anything right.' 'I should just retire and have done with it.' She noticed these thoughts were getting in the way of her teaching and she was getting behind with her work. She felt tired all the time. But also, she thought she needed to do more and more at work to prove she was still capable. She often worked well into the night planning lessons and ensuring things were done.

Keeping busy also helped her feel distracted from her osteoporosis and from the fact she had let other areas of her life slip. Sarah also noticed that she did not want to go out and see her friends anymore. She did not have the energy or time and thought that she would not enjoy it. She could not see any point in contacting them.

She found it increasingly difficult to concentrate at work. This made her feel even worse, thinking over and over, 'I am a failure.' Things started to get worse and the exam results of children in her class dropped.

Finally, when she felt unable to go to work, Sarah went to her GP to discuss her difficulties.

Given the way she was feeling, her GP recommended she take some time off work. He also recommended that she went to see the local IAPT service that would support her using CBT. He made her an appointment at the service for an assessment.

Sarah attended an assessment with Emily, a Psychological Wellbeing Practitioner (PWP). Emily explained how there are links between how you feel physically, your thoughts and what you do as a result. These can form a vicious circle that can keep you feeling down. Emily explained that breaking into this circle using CBT self-help can help to reverse it and make you feel better.

Sarah was attracted to this approach and felt it applied to her. She wondered if her lack of concentration would get in the way of using the self-help techniques, however. Emily said it may be difficult at first, but the support she would receive would help motivate her to get started. She explained that the CBT self-help book was written in a straightforward way. It would take her through treatment step-by-step, and she would be in control of it. Emily also said the key CBT technique they would use was called behavioural activation (we come to this in Section 3). Rather than 'thinking her way out of depression' the focus was on 'acting her way out of depression'. Emily explained they would do this by building routine and structure back into her daily life. It would get her back to the things she was avoiding as a result of how she felt. Sandra thought this sounded ideal. See how Sandra got on with CBT self-help in Section 5 from page 145.

Q&A

Bill and Sarah's stories show more about the ways in which people experience depression differently. You may still have questions about low mood or depression and why it has happened to you. We will try to answer some of the most commonly asked questions people have about depression.

Question 1: What is depression?

Depression is a general term that covers a range of different types and levels of severity of mood problems. People with depression often find that they have a number of commonly experienced symptoms such as:

- Feeling down, low or sad
- Feeling hopeless and helpless

- Tearfulness

- Being more irritable and less tolerant of others

- Having no motivation or interest in things

- Finding it difficult to make decisions

- Problems concentrating

- Moving or speaking more slowly than usual

- Change in appetite or weight (increased or decreased)

- Constipation

- Unexplained aches and pains

- A lack of energy

- Decreased sex drive

- Changes to sleep (problems getting off to sleep or staying asleep, waking up earlier than normal, or sleeping more than usual)

- Avoiding contact with friends, family and social contacts

- Neglecting hobbies and interests.

Depression may be mild, moderate or severe, depending on the number of symptoms someone is experiencing and the impact those symptoms are having on the person's life.

There is still a lot of debate among mental health professionals about what causes depression and low mood. There are various theories that propose that depression may be either caused by genetic factors, environmental factors or personal losses. While these theories may be true, it is likely that most people become depressed due to a combination of them. You may recognise a trigger for your own low mood or depression. But it may not be easy to pin it down to any one thing. You may not be able to think of anything. Depression, like other illnesses, can just happen.

What is known, however, is that depression affects people of all different ages, cultures and social classes. At any one time, one in four people experience problems like depression or anxiety. This figure shows how common it is to experience depression (or depression and anxiety together).

Depression is so widely experienced that sometimes it has been called the 'common cold of mental health problems'. This phrase fails to do justice to the impact it can have on people's lives and how serious it is. Having depression is a very personal and difficult experience for anyone to go through. Getting the right support at the right time is really important. We know from our own clinical and personal experience that having depression is serious and that it can be helped.

The NHS Choices website has excellent resources to find out more about depression. This includes a video that outlines the symptoms of depression, early warning signs and what can be done about it. You can watch it with the following link: http://www.nhs.uk/Conditions/Depression/Pages/Introduction.aspx.

The Charity MIND have also created excellent resources about what depression is. They have an excellent video where people share what depression was like for them and their own journeys using CBT treatments: http://www.mind.org.uk/information-support/types-of-mental-health-problems/depression.

Question 2: Why me?

As you will have read above, this is really difficult to answer. There is no simple explanation as to why some people develop depression and others do not. Depression can affect people at any age and from any walk of life. Some people may be able to recognise a key event (or events) that started them feeling this way. These might be the death of a loved one or losing a job. Others may not be able to pick out any particular thing that happened around the time their low mood started.

However, everyone who experiences depression or low mood reports changes to their physical wellbeing, their thinking and what they do. These are the things we can do something about, using this CBT self-help book. In some ways it doesn't matter how you ended up here. What matters is finding out what may be keeping your depression going and what you can do about it. It will help you both now and in the future, if you begin to feel this way again. Working through this book and putting it into action will help you overcome your depression.

Question 3: Why does depression feel like it has taken over my whole life?

People with depression often say that depression affects three main areas of their life:

1. Changes in their behaviour (what they do or not do as a result)

People with depression say that they notice they may be doing much less of some things they used to do. They find they avoid and stop certain things that are difficult because of their symptoms. People may also find they do more of certain things to try and feel better. They may sleep more for example, eat more or find they spend more money. All of these changes are understandable. They are trying to manage how they are feeling and get some initial short-term relief. In the longer term, though, these changes cause more problems and keep their mood spiralling down.

2. Changes to their thinking (negative thoughts and ruminating)

People find that the thoughts going through their mind become more negative. These thoughts can go round and round, and be hard to stop or switch off. They may also find they have negative thoughts about being unwell and the depression itself. This is all known as rumination. Sometimes people try to manage negative thinking by pushing the thoughts out of their mind or using distraction. This actually backfires, causing more negative thoughts. Negative thoughts can impact on how the person feels physically and also what they do as a result. When people avoid things or have physical symptoms, that can also lead to further negative thoughts, it keeps the spiral of low mood going round.

3. Changes in how they feel physically (changes within the body)

People with depression notice a range of physical changes. Sometimes they notice these first before they realise they are feeling depressed. People frequently report feeling tired and exhausted, that they struggle to concentrate, and have changes to their appetite and to sleep patterns. People may also notice more aches and pains, headaches or other physical problems. These symptoms are understandably hard to manage. They can lead to changes in what the person does and their thinking, keeping that spiral going down.

One thing leads to another, and these three areas each have a knock-on effect on the other. This makes it feel like depression has taken over your whole life. It creates a vicious circle and keeps mood spiralling down. Jane's experiences are described in the diagram opposite. You may not be experiencing all the same things as she did, but if your mood is low you will probably recognise your own changes in these areas.

Jane's changes in behaviour

Not meeting my friend Sally for coffee

Avoiding opening letters

Stop going out with my husband for meals/drinks

Staying in bed longer

Off sick from work

Eating junk food which is quick to prepare

Jane's negative thoughts

'I will never get better'

'There is no point going out as I am not good company'

'People will not want to see me like this'

'I am useless'

'I am letting my family down'

'I am a failure at work'

'I cannot be bothered'

Jane's physical changes

Tiredness, problems sleeping, tearfulness, headaches, weight gain, problems concentrating, being irritable with my husband and children

Tiredness can stop people doing things they need or want to do. This can lead to initial relief from tiredness in the short term, but in the long term can lead to negative thoughts. Problems concentrating can result in negative thoughts like 'I can't do anything properly any more'. This can then result in taking time off work and spending more time in bed. Each area has a knock-on effect on the other.

This 'downward spiral' is called the vicious circle of depression. It maintains low mood and is hard to break out of when it has taken hold. For example, depression may make it difficult for you to go to work, or concentrate if you are there. Or it may affect your relationship with others around you. These symptoms all get better through the right treatment and the vicious circle of depression can be broken.

Question 4: What can be done about depression?

The good news is that there are a number of things that can be done about depression. Some evidence-based treatments are described below. These are treatments that have been researched extensively and are known to work for many people who use them.

CBT self-help

This is how we are working here. It is recommended by the National Institute for Health and Care Excellence (NICE) as a result of its good evidence base. The approach is based on cognitive behavioural therapy (CBT), a time-limited, active psychological therapy that gives you the tools to help yourself. You can use CBT self-help without support from someone else (like buying a self-help book and using it, or using a computerised CBT website). However, having someone for support who encourages and motivates you to use it can be really effective. This is recommended as it has been shown it can make it more effective. This could be a friend, family member or a professional. This support is especially helpful if you find yourself struggling with the motivation or concentration to use it. Support should provide encouragement to help keep you on track if you are experiencing any difficulties using the self-help. If you think you would benefit from support to use this approach, ask your GP about what is available in your area. If you are in England you can find local services and how to self-refer here: http://www.iapt.nhs.uk/services/. What is good about CBT self-help is that it is flexible, effective and can fit around you and your life. If someone is being supported to use CBT self-help this can be done flexibly too: face-to-face with a practitioner, over the telephone or via internet/email.

Psychological therapies/counselling

Some people attend regular sessions face-to-face with a therapist or counsellor who provides treatment to help them overcome depression. There are currently a range of psychological therapies that are provided in this way. However, there can be waiting lists due to the demand for treatment for depression. The availability of services varies tremendously by area.

If you feel that you need more support or this type of approach, it is important to ask for a psychological therapy for depression that is recommended by NICE. Within NICE guidelines for depression, CBT is the treatment of choice people should be offered first. Interpersonal therapy (IPT), brief dynamic interpersonal psychotherapy (DIT), Behavioural Couples Counselling or 10 sessions of counselling are also recommended by NICE for depression for people who do not benefit from CBT. It is also important that the person is fully trained and accredited. You should ask to see their training and accreditation certificates to check they are a member of the right professional body.

Antidepressant medication

There are also a range of different antidepressant medications available for depression. Your GP may suggest starting an antidepressant medication if they think your depression is moderate to severe in level. They are not usually given for mild depression. CBT works well with medication and the two things can be used in combination. Research has shown this to be effective. If you are taking a medication for depression you should take it as prescribed. Your GP will let you know how long you should take it for. Usually the first medication that is prescribed is from a group of medications called SSRIs (selective serotonin reuptake inhibitors). You can find more information about medications for depression on the NHS Choices website here: http://www.nhs.uk/conditions/ssris-(selective-serotonin-reuptake-inhibitors)/Pages/Introduction.aspx.

Antidepressants can take several weeks to build up in the body and reach an effective level. Equally, they reduce down in the body slowly once they are stopped. This means people sometimes stop taking their medication too soon when they start to feel better. When the effects of the medication wear off they feel down again. Therefore, if at any point you want to stop taking your medication, always discuss it with your GP first. They will know how long they advise you remain on it after you feel better to ensure your mood stabilises. They will also advise you on a safe way of stopping it gradually. It is important that you do not just stop taking the medication without first telling your GP of your plans. There is also a great deal of misunderstanding about antidepressant medication. Sometimes people do not want to take them as they think they are addictive or that they cause weight gain. This is not the case. It is important to make an informed decision by getting information from a reputable source, like the NHS Choices website. Taking medication or not is a personal choice. Some people choose not to have medication and use CBT self-help or other talking treatments instead. The important thing is to be well informed. Get good information about the medication, its side effects and how it works.

Question 5: Will it happen again?

It is important to be honest here. Depression can happen again to some, but not all people. Research shows us that about 50 per cent of people who have had a single episode of depression will not go on to experience it again. The other 50 per cent, however, may become depressed again in the future. There is no currently agreed way of knowing who will have another episode in the future.

But there are things that can be done to reduce the chances of it happening. The good news is that people who learn to identify their early warning signs for depression can help themselves to stay well by putting their CBT techniques into practice again.

We know that having depression is an awful experience to go through. Some people who have been depressed before may see getting depressed again as a major failure or setback, thinking 'everything is back to square one'. They can become anxious about fluctuations in their mood and see these as a sign they are slipping back. In fact, it is normal for us to have good days and bad days. Learning that mood fluctuations are OK is an important part of staying well. Mood will fluctuate on a day-by-day basis as these ups and downs are a part of everyday life.

In Section 4, you will learn how to create a relapse prevention toolkit and to monitor your mood once you are feeling better. This means that should you have another episode, or any early warning signs of one, you will know what action to take. This will hopefully ensure that any episode is headed off at the pass.

The tools and techniques that you will learn in this self-help book are lifelong skills. You will be able to take control over your mood when you need to.

How is your own depression or low mood affecting you?

We have so far explored how depression affects us physically, our thoughts and what we do (or don't do) as a result. Now it is time to apply this new understanding to your own situation. Like the example on page 45, fill in the three areas on the diagram opposite.

1. What physical changes have you noticed since feeling this way? Write these in the **physical** box.

2. Next, think about how feeling this way has affected what you are doing. In **behaviours**, make a note of those things that you are doing more of because of the symptoms you are experiencing. Then note the things you are doing less of or have stopped altogether as a result of how you feel.

3. Then consider how your thinking has changed. Are you experiencing more negative thoughts? What are the thoughts you notice? In **thoughts**, add some examples of any changes to your thinking you have noticed at times you feel down.

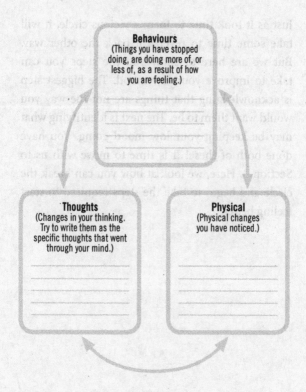

Behaviours
(Things you have stopped doing, are doing more of, or less of, as a result of how you are feeling.)

Thoughts
(Changes in your thinking. Try to write them as the specific thoughts that went through your mind.)

Physical
(Physical changes you have noticed.)

These three areas interact and cause a vicious circle of depression or low mood that keeps spiralling down. They all impact upon each other, creating a knock-on effect. But there is good news. Breaking into this circle in one of the areas will help to reverse it. This in turn will help you to begin to feel better.

Just as it took time to form a vicious circle, it will take some time to reverse it back the other way. But we are here to show you the steps you can take to improve your low mood. The biggest step is acknowledging that things are not the way you would want them to be. The next is identifying what may be keeping your low mood going. You have done both of these! It is time to move with us to Section 3. Here, we look at how you can break the circle and begin to take the steps required to start feeling better.

BEHAVIOURAL ACTIVATION

If you have completed sections 1 and 2, well done! We hope you have found useful information about depression and how common it is. And that you are reassured there are evidence-based treatments that can help. We are really pleased that you have stayed with us and the book so far.

You may have turned straight to this section, as you are keen to get going or already know enough about depression. In the last section we explained about the vicious circle of depression. We helped you identify your own symptoms and how this personally affects you. If you haven't done that, it will help to turn back to page 53 and fill in your symptoms, as these will be your target for treatment using the techniques below. You may also want to set goals for treatment. You can complete your goals on page 23.

Now it is time to tackle breaking into your own vicious circle of low mood or depression. In this section we are going to work together to beat how you are currently feeling using behavioural activation (BA). You will learn more about BA and how it works, and make a plan to put your own BA into action.

Key point

Remember you are in control. If you are not sure about anything in the book, you can always go back through it again. Fold the corner of pages you mean to come back to at a time to suit you. Highlighting things that stand out for you can help too. Don't be afraid of writing in the book or making notes, that's what it is for! Remember the key thing is to put BA into action in your own life to feel better.

What is BA?

Behavioural activation, or BA for short, is a CBT technique that is recommended by NICE for depression. A great deal of research has been undertaken on BA which has shown it to be effective. Just as importantly, many people with depression have told us how helpful BA is in helping them to feel better. BA helps you to build back a balance of routine, necessary and pleasurable activities to break the vicious circle of depression. It does this by getting the person to do activities based on an external plan rather than how they are thinking or feeling inside.

Main features of BA

BA helps people by:

- Building back a routine in their daily life.

- Getting the right balance of activities we all need in our week.

- Helping people to act according to external activity targets, rather than how they are thinking or feeling internally. (In other words, acting according to a goal, not a thought or feeling.) This breaks the vicious circle of depression and can stop it forming again in the future.

- Engages people in tasks that are planned in advance which in turn reduces negative thinking.

- Working in a graded way, at a pace that suits you, tackling easier things first.

BA does not require you to concentrate for long periods of time or think too much about things. It is a 'doing' treatment. As the old adage goes, you can act your way out of depression, but not think your way out of it. It is also taken at a pace to suit you, and that you feel in control of. You will do just one or two things a week differently to begin with, then build up gradually.

How does BA break the vicious circle?

When we are depressed we tend to withdraw from activities and people around us. We find that our daily routine slips. Necessary things, which have important consequences if we do not do them, become harder to do. We reduce or stop things that we used to enjoy or value. Sometimes we manage to keep doing some necessary things, such as going to work or providing care for children or loved ones. In fact, we may even do more of those things to try and feel better. But the things we personally value or enjoy – like hobbies, interests and socialising, for example – slip away. We become out of balance.

Avoiding things that have become difficult as a result is understandable. Not doing these things might help in the short term. Doing less may actually make you feel better and give some relief from those symptoms. In the longer term, however, avoidance becomes unhelpful and actually makes mood worse. It takes you away from the things that give you positive feedback, like hobbies and interests, seeing friends and socialising. It also means you don't get things done that need to be completed.

Your routine changes and things build up more and more. People notice they have more negative thoughts as a result of doing less and not being involved in activities. These negative thoughts can keep going round and round in your mind (rumination). All of these together can lead to more physical symptoms, even more avoidance and your mood becoming still lower. The negative circle goes round and round, spiralling mood down further.

Behavioural activation breaks the vicious circle by putting it into reverse. By taking small steps, you start to feel better and have more energy and confidence to take the next step. Best of all, you are the one who sets the pace. You are the person who will decide what to do and when. You will be doing things according to your goals and targets, not how you are thinking or feeling internally. Over time, mood lifts and the circle is broken.

When people feel low they have physical symptoms such as tiredness and low motivation, as well as negative thoughts.

As a result, they begin to avoid activities, which initially gives some relief from the burden of doing them.

Understandably the short term relief leads to further avoidance of activites

The avoidance means that they get behind with the things that need doing, are unable to find the energy to do the things they used to do every day, and do fewer things they used to enjoy or value.

Doing fewer things, they may notice more negative and unhelpful thoughts that keep going round and round their minds.

Their mood drops even further, making their symptoms even worse.

The most important thing to remember about BA: outside-in not inside-out!

The most important thing to remember is that to break that vicious circle you do activities 'outside-in'. rather than 'inside-out'.

When feeling low, we can often slip into a circle of doing things (or not doing them) because of what we are thinking or feeling inside (what's inside us affecting what we do outside). Initially, it may give you some relief from how you are feeling. In the longer term, avoiding things because of how you are feeling or thinking inside takes you away from your routine and the things you used to enjoy. Things that you need to do mount up and can feel harder and harder to tackle. This leads to further avoidance, more negative thoughts and more physical symptoms, keeping that vicious circle spiralling down.

BA uses an **outside-in** approach. This means, instead of doing (or not doing) activities based on how you feel or think inside, you do activities based on an outside plan. You set a target activity, an outside goal that is planned ahead in advance. You carry out the planned task despite how you are feeling on that day or any off-putting thoughts you may have.

Getting going with BA

Just thinking about getting going again may seem overwhelming. You may be struggling with low energy levels and tiredness.. For example, you may be thinking, 'How can I get on with BA when I already feel tired?' If this thought is going through your mind, try to recognise it just as one of those off-putting thoughts. Following it would be acting from the inside-out, and we are trying to break that pattern. You may also be thinking that BA sounds too easy, wondering 'How can this possibly help?' We ask you to try it a few times: see what happens. Remember it takes time to reverse that vicious circle, but it does reverse. BA as a CBT technique has worked for many, many people with depression. It is recommended as a stand-alone treatment that people should be offered. We have worked with hundreds of people who have used BA and felt better. If you are wondering if it is right for you, all we ask is that you try it for a few weeks. We are hopeful that it can help, and that's based on our clinical experience and research evidence. If it has worked for the many people we have worked with, then hopefully it can work for you too.

If it seems overwhelming to imagine getting back to doing things when you feel like this, remember: BA goes at a pace to suit you and is done in a graded way. You choose the activities you begin with that are easier and feel manageable. You are not expected to get back to the more difficult things straight away. Initially you will only do a couple of things per week, that's all we ask.

Key point

Initially, you may not feel the same achievement or enjoyment from tasks that you used to. Remember, this is not the aim at first. It will take a while to reverse that vicious circle and for your feelings to return to what they were before. Your mood will start to lift as you progress through the treatment, but don't expect it to happen straightaway. The aim of BA is just to start doing things again to break that vicious circle. The goal is to build back your routine, targeting activities you are avoiding and getting a balance of activities. Have confidence that your mood will lift as this happens. Remember, you are working to the outside goal or target on your BA diary, not to how you are thinking or feeling.

The steps of BA

Now we are going to make a plan together to help you to beat your own low mood or depression using BA.

BA works in 4 steps:

Step 1: Identify a list of activities that you are avoiding or have stopped altogether because of how you are feeling. There are three types of activities you should list:

    a) Routine – things you do regularly

    b) Necessary – things where there would be an important consequence if you don't do them

    c) Pleasurable – things that you used to previously enjoy or value doing.

Step 2: Grade the activities on a hierarchy from the most difficult through to easier ones. Make sure you have the three types of activities in each section.

Step 3: Make a plan in a diary to do some easier tasks over the next few days. Carry them out using the outside-in approach.

Step 4: Reflect on how it went. Make a new plan to do more activities on your list.

Now we'll look at these in more detail.

Step 1: Identify activities you are avoiding

This important first step aims to identify things that you are avoiding. To do this, think about things that you have stopped doing or reduced since feeling low or depressed. In the following worksheet, write in all the ones that you can think of. There are some tips to help you to identify activities on page 70.

You probably won't be able to fill in all the activities in one go. Begin with those that first come to mind, and then return to the list later on.

Identifying my avoided activities worksheet

Activities I am avoiding as a result of how I feel		
Things that I do routinely (Washing-up, hoovering, grocery shopping, etc.)	Things that I used to enjoy or value (Hobbies, interests, sociable occasions, etc.)	Things that are necessary, or there will be important consequences (Paying bills, taking prescribed medication, etc.)

Tips for identifying activities

Your values

Sometimes when we are low it can be hard to recall things we used to enjoy. Try to think back to a time when you were happier in life and really visualise it in your mind. Where were you, what was going on around you? What was it about that time you valued? This can help you to generate more things to add to your list.

You can also add activities that you have always wanted to do, but have not done before. Perhaps a new hobby you have always wanted to try. Make it personal to you.

There may be reasons why something you enjoyed before isn't as easy to do any more. It may seem impossible due to a physical health problem. Perhaps the person you used to do the activity you enjoyed with is not around any more. If this is the case for you, try and think of what mattered most about that activity, its value to you. What was it you enjoyed about it and valued? Was it being outdoors, spending time with someone you care about, spending time for yourself? Sometimes we cannot do an activity in the same way any more. But we can do other things that bring us closer to what we valued from it. It all helps us to break that vicious circle. For example, if you enjoyed a sport but have an injury that means you cannot play in the same way as you did before, you can work out what you valued from the activity. This could be the competitiveness or being in a group. Then think about what other activities you could still do that would give you a sense of competition or being in a social group. While they may not be the same as the sport you really enjoyed, getting back to the things you valued about it is a really helpful way of breaking the circle.

Your senses

The longer that vicious circle has been going around, the more difficult it can be to think of anything you used to enjoy. Activities you put into your list don't have to just be big things you do at home or with other people. You can put smaller, more personal activities on your list too and things that are inexpensive or free. A really good way to generate things for your list is to think about your senses. Each of us probably has a taste we like, or a favourite sound or smell for example. Try using each of your senses to help you to generate more things to put on your list.

- Think about your favourite sounds, maybe a piece of music, birdsong or the sounds of the leaves blowing in the wind. Whatever is personal to you.

- What about your favourite smell? Is there a way of putting that on your list? It could be the smell of a certain flower or something in your home. You could cook, creating your favourite aroma, or wear your favourite perfume/aftershave again. Whatever your favourite smell is, find a way to put it on your list.

- What about your favourite view or image? You may be able to go and see it or there may be pictures you could look at online or in photographs.

- Similarly think of your favourite taste, something you really enjoyed eating before.

- Put this on your list, too, and any others that come to mind.

Building back a routine

Look at the list of activities that you have created. Have you put everyday routine activities on this list? For instance, trying to get up at the same time each day rather than staying in bed past a certain time.

Eating regularly through the day and going to bed at the same time each night count too. Remember building back a routine will help to break that circle, so add these too if you haven't already.

Is it a routine or necessary thing?

Sometimes it can be difficult to know whether to put something in the routine column or the necessary one. It can seem like everything needs to be done. Necessary things in BA are where there will be consequences in the short term as a result if you don't do them. For example, not sorting out a direct debit for your mortgage or paying bills, or a diabetic avoiding taking their insulin.

If you have a physical illness or injury

If you have a physical illness or injury that is affecting you completing your list, these strategies may help you.

Having a physical illness or injury may affect you being able to do the things that you used to enjoy. It is easy to give up and stop your hobbies and interests as a result. It can be hard to see a way through to being able to do them. If this is the case for you, then we know how difficult and very upsetting this can be. We have worked with many people who have had depression and life-limiting illnesses or long-term conditions that have affected them being able to do things in the same way they did before. We want to share a technique called SOC that has helped them and other people in this situation.

SOC is a technique that is often used when working with people who have physical problems in later life. It is also used by sports people when they are injured and cannot do their full training or can no longer do their sport in the same way. It keeps them doing something, even if it isn't the exact same thing they would be doing without the injury.

A good example of this is at the gym. If, say, you injure your left arm, you would not be able to do your usual exercises that use the left arm muscles. But you may be able to select down the exercises that you do, focusing on other parts of the body. Practising those specific exercises more may mean you get better at them and grow stronger. You might compensate for the injury by, for example, wearing a support on the injured arm.

The SOC technique has three parts:

- **Select it down:** select down parts of the activity you may be able to do.

- **Optimise it:** doing the things that you have selected should optimise your experience of them.

- **Compensate for it:** is there a way you could compensate for the illness or injury to still carry it out?

Another example is an artist who had developed early stages of osteoarthritis in his hand. He adapted what he did to continue to paint. First he selected down the amount of time he would paint for and when. His pain and stiffness was worse in the mornings, so he would start his day slightly later when this had eased off. Then, instead of painting for long periods of time without a break, he built in short breaks every hour.

He also selected down the work he would take on. Instead of taking on lots of large oil commissions, he took on smaller oils and increased the number of watercolours that he took on. He found these easier to paint and less stressful on his hand. That meant his income wasn't affected as they took less time each to complete. And because he was painting more watercolours he found his work got better in that medium and got great feedback.

To compensate for the arthritis, he wore a wrist and hand splint when he needed it. He also found special foam rings for his brushes that allowed him to get a better grip.

You are the expert in the activity that you used to enjoy. If it applies to you, try and think through ways to use this technique to get back to doing the activity. Of course always check it out first with your GP, physiotherapist or anyone else involved in your care, as necessary.

Can you **select down** parts of the activity to still do some of it but not all? For example, you could select certain parts of your gardening that you enjoy and are still manageable. Or you could select down the exercises in your routine so that you are still training but avoiding the injury.

This means you would do a selected part of the activity, but may do that more often. Doing this may help to **optimise** your experience of it. People often find that by practising a selection of a task they get better at it.

Is there anything that you can add in to help make it easier and **compensate** for the injury or pain? For example a splint, physio, massage or similar? It may be adapting what you do in some way and adding in something practical to help.

Sarah, who you met in Section 1, used SOC to help her to create her avoided activities list. It helped her get back to activities she used to enjoy that had been affected by her osteoporosis diagnosis. You can read more about how she did this in Section 5 from page 147.

Remember, you are the expert in the activity you used to do, be it golf, exercise, cooking or something else. If you have a physical limitation or illness, see if SOC can help you to keep that activity on your list.

If you cannot do something at all any more?

Sometimes, physical health problems or an illness mean that we are prevented from doing an activity we enjoyed. This can be frustrating and devastating, and can lead people to give up on a range of other things too. That important balance of activities starts to slip and it can affect mood too.

If you think this applies to you, think about what you can still do instead. Think about what you need to add to the worksheet to have a routine and balance of activities. How might you be able to do this? Are there other sensory- or values-based activities you could do, such as the ones suggested above?

If you have are having treatment or in hospital it can be hard to think past the treatment. It can be scary to make plans ahead as you may have to cancel or rearrange them. You may be too unwell to do them when the times comes around. This can make things hard and challenging for you, but also can keep you in that vicious circle. Sometimes people with cancer or other life-limiting physical problems find it hard to make plans or set goals, as it is hard to know what the future may entail. If this applies to you then we would encourage you to think about your values of the activity you cannot do. Is there something you can do in the next few days, weeks and months (or whatever timeframe you feel comfortable with) that you can add to your list?

For example, one thing you valued about an activity might be that you shared it with a friend or loved one. Can you find ways to spend time with them in a different way? Can you Skype them from hospital or ring them? Can you arrange for them to spend some time with you and bring a game or activity you could do together? Think carefully about the thing you can no longer do and use the values exercise to work out what you valued about it.

For example, Julie had a cancer diagnosis and was having chemotherapy treatment. This meant being in hospital for it each week and side effects like tiredness and sickness. She had lost her hair and felt self-conscious about this. Prior to her chemotherapy, Julie and her husband would always take the children for a family day out each weekend. They would surprise the children with a new place each week. They'd give them clues on the way so they could try and guess where they were headed. Since becoming ill, they had not been able to do the trip regularly. Julie's hospital appointments and tiredness got in the way, but also Mark was working different hours to cover childcare and Julie's appointments.

Due to her health, Julie could not manage long trips in the car or lots of time away from home. But what she valued most about those trips wasn't the places they went to particularly. It was the sense of fun of all four of them doing something together and guessing. She valued surprising her children and seeing them look so happy. She also valued spending time together as a family with her husband Mark and having time together each week.

She discussed this with Mark. They decided that instead of trips out, another family activity that they could do together would be to have a family film night. This was shorter and felt manageable, so even if Julie wasn't feeling very well she could still join them. They built a den on the sofa with duvets for the children. Mark made popcorn and large drinks with straws. Julie was able to lie down and watch the film with everyone snuggled up together. They would all take it in turns to choose the film and the others had to guess what it was. After the film Mark would do a quiz for everyone with questions. 'What colour was the waiter's shirt?' 'How many people were in the lift scene?' They really enjoyed it and it brought them together as a family in a different way. The children loved being able to spend quality time with their mum again.

While the activity you do may not be the same (and we appreciate this can be challenging), you are building balance back in by doing something. BA is often used with people with long-term health conditions. It can lift your mood and help you to live better with your physical health problem or illness.

Step 2: Grade your avoided activities on your BA hierarchy worksheet

You have now identified as many routine, necessary and pleasurable activities as you can think of. The next step is to make a **hierarchy**. The aim of the hierarchy is so that you can do BA in a **graded** way. A hierarchy is putting your Step 1 activities into the order of how difficult they are to do at the moment.

To do this, start by taking the list of routine activities. Rate them as most difficult, medium difficulty and less difficult, which you feel you could tackle straight away. If the activity seems almost impossible for you to do at the moment, write it under **most difficult**. If the activities would be difficult but do not seem impossible, write them under **medium difficulty**. Those you feel you could possibly manage in the next week or so place under **less difficult**. It is possible that those you feel are least difficult may still be challenging however.

It is important to do this section by section from your avoided activities list. When you have completed your routine activities, rate your necessary activities list, then your pleasurable ones. On the hierarchy you should have a **balance of routine things, necessary things and pleasurable things in each section**. You will then have a balance of activities when you start to carry out your BA tasks in Step 3.

To help, there are some tips for grading your activities below.

My BA hierarchy

Think about the tasks you identified on your avoided activities list. Working through each part of the list, routine, necessary and pleasurable, transfer them into the three sections below. Put R, N or P to identify it in the column on the right can help you to see the balance visually. Remember there should be a mix of all three types of activities in each section of the hierarchy.

There are blank copies of the hierarchy worksheets in further resources, on page 170, should you need more.

Tips for grading your activities

If everything seems difficult

If you find it difficult to identify any less difficult activities, a helpful tip is to try and break the activities down in your other sections. Look at the activities you have identified as most difficult or medium difficulty. Think about ways you could break these activities down into smaller ones. For example, say you have put 'cook dinner on a Sunday' as a most difficult task. Break this down into smaller tasks leading up to it, such as planning the menu and shopping for food, etc. Rather than saying clean the whole house, break this into tasks such as hoovering, for example. Then break the hoovering down further, into rooms.

DIFFICULTY	ACTIVITY		R	N	P
Most difficult					
Medium difficulty					
Less difficult					

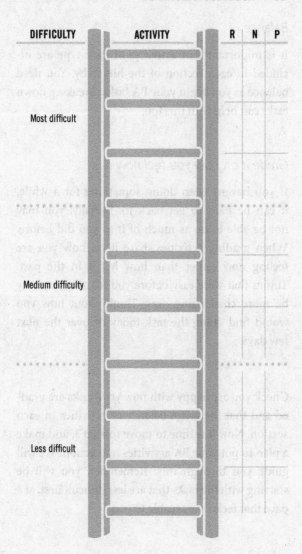

Balance

It is important that activities of each type are in-cluded in each section of the hierarchy. You need balance as you begin your BA tasks. Breaking down tasks can help with this too.

Grade it on how you feel now

If you haven't been doing something for a while, it can be hard to get back to. Initially, you may not be able to do as much of it as you did before. When grading activities, base it on how you are feeling now rather than how it felt in the past. Things that were easy before you felt this way may be more challenging now. Think about how you would find doing the task today or over the next few days.

Check you are happy with how your tasks are grad-ed and that there is a balance of activities in each section. Now it is time to move to Step 3, and make a plan to put your BA activities into action. We will guide you through this. Remember, you will be starting with the tasks that are less difficult first, at a pace that feels manageable to you.

Step 3: Put your hierarchy into action

The next step is to pick some activities from the less difficult section on your hierarchy. You will plan to do these over the next week. You won't be doing all of them at once. Just one or two for the first week is perfect – a maximum of three, depending on how you are feeling. You will transfer these into your BA planning diary.

You may feel that you could get more done than this – don't. BA is about planning things to do that give balance across the week and then doing them. Using outside-in, you do them despite how you may be feeling at that time or any negative thoughts you have. It is important not to take on too much in the early stages of BA. Activities will build up as you progress with it.

You also need to consider if there are any necessary tasks you need to complete in this coming week. Things that have a deadline or have an immediate consequence. See the box below for how to tackle this.

Putting a necessary task into action

When putting your hierarchy into action, you should try to start off with the less difficult activities. However, look at the necessary activities column on your hierarchy – ones where there may be consequences if they are not done. These are activities that may need to be prioritised. If you notice that something needs to be done soon, think about ways you could do it. It might be paying an important overdue bill or getting your car taxed before it runs out.

It may be that these things are in your most difficult section. If so, see if there is a way you can break the task down to a pace to suit you. For example, if you needed to get a tax disk the steps could be:

- Reading through the reminder and finding what information you need to give

- Finding your logbook

- Planning a time to go to the post office or the car tax website.

Put the steps you choose onto your hierarchy, and if the deadline is approaching put these in your planning diary.

To ensure you don't do too much, if you do a necessary task, do one less from your less difficult list. Remember, you are aiming for a maximum of three tasks across the week, spread out over the seven days.

Putting activities into your planning diary

When you put activities in your diary, it is important to think about where you are putting them. Initially, space out your activities across the week instead of doing more than one thing on the same day. When writing them down, make your plan as specific as possible. If you plan to read the newspaper:

- State **which** paper you are going to read

- **Where** you plan to read it

- **When** you are going to do it and

- Whether you need anyone **with** you to do it.

Visualising doing these things – the which, where, when and with whom – can really help you to plan it out. It helps you to think through anything that may block or get in the way of your plan. And means it is more likely you will do it.

Things that could get in the way

Consider the time of day you put things in your diary. Does it work around other commitments or things that will be happening? Does it involve a first step that you hadn't thought about until now – like going to buy a paper? These things can feel overwhelming if not thought through in advance and planned. If so, go back to your hierarchy and add in the missing step and plan to do that first. It's OK to break that first step down further too.

Internal things

Sometimes things within us can get in the way of our plans. This could be:

- Your confidence
- How much you understand about what you are doing and why you are doing it
- Off-putting thoughts
- Physical symptoms.

If there is something you feel could get in the way of your plan, like your physical symptoms, tiredness or off-putting thoughts, how will you overcome it? Remember the main focus of BA is to act outside-in and not act because of those thoughts or feelings inside you.

If you don't feel confident to do your plan, is it graded enough? Is there something that would be less difficult to do first? Use the tips below to help you to do this. Remember, negative thoughts can try and push you into not doing your plan. Do it anyway and you are in control of what you do rather than having your thoughts control you. How do you know you can't do something unless you try? Stick to that external goal you have planned.

You might find you are not sure why you are doing BA or if this approach will work for you. If so, re-visit your goals on page 23. It can also help to turn back to 'Building motivation to change' on page 19. Visualise again what life will be like in five years' time if BA does work for you. Remember, it has worked for many other people. If there is something you are unsure about, turn back to that page in the book. Read through how BA works again, and the steps to carrying it out. You are always in control.

External things

Sometimes things happen that are outside of our control that get in the way of the best-laid plans. These external things sometimes cannot be helped.

Neighbours turn up, or the phone rings, or there are childcare problems. Are there any things that you think may happen at the times you have planned to do your activities? A certain person who tends to drop over or ring at that time, children's bedtime, etc.? If so, is there a better time you could plan your activity in?

Often though, these things are not possible to predict and plan for in advance. They are outside of us and outside of our control. If something gets in the way of your planned activity, just reschedule it. Decide what you are going to do and when you are going to do it and pop it into your diary. That way, you can still carry on with your plan at a more suitable time. Make sure that you only do this for external things that get in the way, though. If it is an internal thought or feeling, remember the main focus of BA is working outside-in.

Key point

You do not need to fill in the rest of the planning diary with other things that you are doing. The other spaces when you are not do-ing a planned BA task remain blank. You will do things during that time – even sitting in a chair is an activity. However, the idea of the diary is that it is a plan in advance, not a record of what you did do.

Tips for carrying out your planned activities in BA

Work outside-in

When it is the time you have planned to do your activity, carry it out. Do it even if you have negative thoughts or symptoms, like tiredness. Remember to work outside-in not inside-out. You may still notice negative thoughts trying to convince you it's too difficult or you will not enjoy it. They are just thoughts, part of your low mood. Letting them control what you do will only keep you acting inside-out. BA will help to reduce those negative thoughts and the impact they have on you. Choose to act against them, do the tasks anyway, working outside-in. Remember, the aim of BA is to do the task, not necessarily to enjoy it straight away. Do the task and those negative thoughts will lose their power and reduce.

Don't overdo it

The aim of BA is not to exhaust yourself from the activity you do. Instead, **leave your energy tank half full**. This may mean not doing as much of the activity as you may have done before you felt low. Stopping before you get too tired to carry on is important. Don't be tempted to do too much if a task goes well. Stick to your plan and stop when you feel you still have enough energy to continue. Then carry on with the rest of your day.

Don't expect too much too soon

Remember the aim of BA is to undo that vicious circle that has taken a while to build up. Reversing it won't happen overnight, but every step is in the right direction. This means that you may not get the same enjoyment or sense of achievement from doing the activity as before. The important thing is to get back to activity and routine. This will break that link between how you are thinking and feeling impacting on what you do.

The first step of BA is to activate according to your planned activity and to keep working through your hierarchy. Your mood will begin to improve once the circle is broken, but how long this takes varies from person to person. You shouldn't expect to feel better just from doing the activities once, it takes a while to reverse that vicious circle. But have confidence that this will happen if you stick with it and keep activating.

Have confidence in the technique and the many people who have felt better by using it. After a few weeks of BA, people often start to notice their mood is improving. Sometimes others around them notice it before they themselves do. Each person is an individual and so will improve at his or her own pace. It isn't a case of the more activities you do, the better you will feel. So don't overload your diary, stick to the advice given above.

Don't forget you are in control

You should go at the pace you want. No one is going to put you under any pressure to go quicker than you want to. Also remember you are not alone. If you are unsure at any time, you can return to the book and see what you need to do. If things do go according to your plan, then you can still learn from the book. Don't give up. Pick the book back up and use the 'Reflecting on my BA plan' worksheet in Step 4 to look at what happened. Then move things forward with a new plan. The great thing about BA is that you can always pick it back up and get going again.

Asking for support

If you are struggling at any time, remember that you can always ask someone you trust for help. They may be able to help by offering you support or encouragement. Or they might help break down parts of necessary tasks that feel just too difficult at the moment. Sometimes when we are low, we take on all the responsibility to get everything done ourselves. If it is too much for you to manage alone, is there someone who could help with a necessary task? Should someone else be doing some of or the entire task? If you feel getting support from a professional would benefit you then contact your GP. If you live in England, you can also contact your local IAPT service, see page 16.

My BA planning diary:
Week 1

Write the planned activities you are going to do in the coming week in the diary on page 96. Add the details of the activity using the questions on the left-hand side. When you have done your activity on the chosen day and time, tick it off to show you have completed it.

There are blank copies of the diary for following weeks that you can use or photocopy in further resources, page 172.

Step 4: Reflect on carrying out the activities and make a new plan

Reflect on how things went

Each week that you do your BA activities, it is important to set aside time afterwards to review how it went. Then you can make a plan for the following week. Use the 'Reflecting on my BA plan worksheet' to identify what you think went well and what you noticed. If you did the activities, did it affect how you felt or what else you did afterwards? Also reflect on days where you did not have an activity planned. Did you do anything different on those days? Or did they feel any different compared to the days when you did have a planned activity? What stands out to you as a result? You can use these reflections to think about which activities from your hierarchy you wish to do next.

What if things didn't go to plan?

If you have struggled with any part of your plan, try to write down what happened. Why didn't things go the way you expected them to? Completing the 'Reflection on my BA plan' worksheet will help identify whether it was an internal or external thing that got in the way. Reviewing may help you think about

My BA planning diary: Week 1

AM	Monday	Tuesday	Wednesday	Thursday	Friday	Saturday	Sunday
What am I going to do?							
When am I doing it?							
Where am I doing it?							
Am I planning to do it with anyone?							

PM	Monday	Tuesday	Wednesday	Thursday	Friday	Saturday	Sunday
What am I going to do?							
When am I doing it?							
Where am I doing it?							
Am I planning to do it with anyone?							

how you can overcome the problem next time. The important thing is to reflect on it and making a new plan to move things forward.

Reflection on my BA plan

There are blank copies of Reflection on my BA plan for following weeks that you can use or photocopy in further resources, page 192.

Reflection on my BA plan

Questions to ask myself about my week	My reflections
If I did my planned BA activities	How did it go?
	What did I notice before I did them?
	What did I notice afterwards?
	Did it impact on what I did for the rest of that day?
	How did it impact upon the next day, and how I felt and what I did as a result?

	What did I notice on the days where I had no planned activity in? Did I think or feel different as a result? What did I do on those days?
	What have I learned as a result of carrying out my BA activities?
	What does this mean for my plan for next week? What do I think I need to do as a result?
If I did not manage to carry out my plan	What stopped me from carrying out my plan?
	Was this an internal problem or an external one?

	How can I overcome this next time?
	What do I think I need to do next week as a result?
Were there any particular times that I noticed myself going over negative things in my mind (ruminating)?	If so, when was this?
	Did this happen when I was engaged in my planned activities or at other times during the week?
	What was I doing at that time?
	How did it impact on what I did and how I felt afterwards?

	What does this teach me about activity and negative thoughts?
	What may be helpful when planning activities next week and where I plan to fit them in as a result of this?

Making a plan for your second week of BA

Now you have reflected on how things have gone, it is time to make a new BA plan for next week. There are more blank diaries at the back of this book, on page 172, that you can use for subsequent weeks. You can photocopy them if you wish to have a larger print copy.

Planning activities for week 2

Turn back to your hierarchy and choose some new activities to do in your second week. Remember what you have learned from your progress this week and keep in mind those main points about BA – getting a balance of activities across the week, acting outside-in and building back your routine.

Choose a mix of routine, necessary and pleasurable tasks across the week and fill them in on page 105. Aim for 2–3 activities, or a maximum of 4. Do less if this feels more manageable or you didn't carry out your BA plan fully last time. These should be spread across your week, not all squeezed together. You should still stick to just one planned activity during a day.

If there is still a pressing necessary task from week 1, you can continue working on this too. Add in any other necessary task on your hierarchy where the deadline is coming during the coming week.

If you didn't manage to do your BA activities last time, you may wish to use those activities again. If they were too much to take on last time and felt overwhelming, break them down further using the tips for planning activities on page 91.

It helps with BA to start to mix activities up to get that balance. For example, if you have a necessary or routine task planned on Monday, on Tuesday you schedule in something pleasurable. Similarly, after a pleasurable task, you should schedule in a routine or necessary task. This reflects the pattern of activities we tend to naturally do when we are not feeling low or depressed.

If you are ruminating

While reflecting on week 1, did you notice that there are particular times or places when you had lots of negative thoughts? When things went round and round in your mind? If so, you may wish to plan to do one of your activities during that time. When you are engaged in an activity, it directly targets rumination. It should help to decrease those negative thoughts and the impact that they have. Over time, BA will help to reduce those thoughts and improve how you feel.

Again, think about any internal or external problems that could get in the way. What can you do to overcome these? For help here, turn back to page 88.

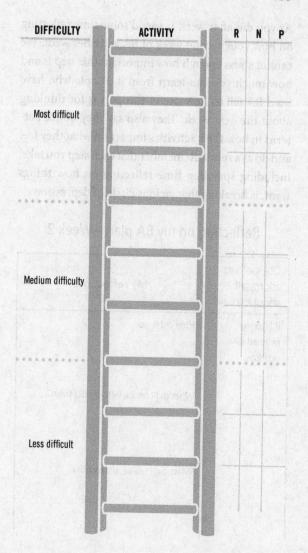

DIFFICULTY	ACTIVITY	R	N	P
Most difficult				
Medium difficulty				
Less difficult				

As you did after week 1, spend some time reflecting on how your second week of BA activities went. We cannot stress enough how important this step is and how much you can learn from it. People who have used BA tell us how useful this part is for thinking about the next week. They also say they notice patterns in how their activities impact on what they feel and do as a result. Remember that each step you take, including spending time reflecting on how things went, is breaking that vicious circle of depression.

Reflection on my BA plan – Week 2

Questions to ask myself about my week	My reflections
If I did my planned BA activities	How did it go? What did I notice before I did them? What did I notice afterwards?

Did it impact on what I did for the rest of that day?

How did it impact upon the next day, and how I felt and what I did as a result?

What did I notice on the days where I had no planned activity in? Did I think or feel different as a result? What did I do on those days?

What have I learned as a result of carrying out my BA activities?

What does this mean for my plan for next week? What do I think I need to do as a result?

If I did not manage to carry out my plan	What stopped me from carrying out my plan?
	Was this an internal problem or an external one?
	How can I overcome this next time?
	What do I think I need to do next week as a result?
Were there any particular times that I noticed myself going over negative things in my mind (ruminating)?	If so, when was this?

Did this happen when I was engaged in my planned activities or at other times during the week?

What was I doing at that time?

How did it impact on what I did and how I felt afterwards?

What does this teach me about my activity and my negative thoughts?

What may be helpful when planning activities next week and where I plan to fit them in as a result of this?

Continuing with BA

When you have completed your reflection for week 2, it is time to plan your third week of BA. There is some advice on planning subsequent weeks of BA below. This includes helping you think about how long to carry out your BA for. Remember, each person is individual. By reflecting after your BA activities each week, you will notice how it impacts on how you are feeling.

As your BA progresses, continue working up your hierarchy of activities. You may wish to start adding more than one activity type per day. This should depend on how your mood is and how realistic this seems. Do not add too much in. You are aiming for balance – also remember to space out your activities to get balance across the week. As in week 2, if you plan to do a necessary or routine task, make the next activity a pleasurable one. Then follow this with another routine or necessary task.

Hopefully you'll find your routine is starting to come back. Aim to eat regularly throughout the day, and get up and go to bed at regular times.

Keep using the 'reflection on my BA plan' worksheets to see how you are progressing and make a plan to go forwards. There are blank diaries and reflection sheets at the back of this book on pages 172–231.

> ### Reminder
>
> Remember the goals you set at the start of this book? Once a month it is important to go back to page 23 and review them. There is more about this below.

How long should you carry on with your BA activities?

As everyone is an individual, we can't predict how many weeks you will need to do your BA activities. You should continue doing BA until you feel you are no longer struggling with the symptoms of depression. For some people this can take four to five weeks, for others it can take 10 weeks or more. There is no right or wrong amount of time you should continue to use BA.

The two main things are to base your decision on are:

1. How your symptoms are improving

2. How far you have moved towards reaching your goals.

Like people often do with antibiotics, it can be tempting to stop as soon as you feel better. We advise that you carry on for at least a few weeks after you start to feel better. Also, make sure that you complete your own relapse prevention toolkit in Section 4. This will help you avoid any lapse in mood becoming more severe.

To help you know when it is time to move on, review your goals and your vicious circle symptoms from the start of treatment.

Consider the main ways in which your symptoms were impacting on each other in your vicious circle, page 53. Have they improved?

Go back to page 23 to re-rate how far you have worked towards your goals. This will help you judge how much progress you have made since starting BA. It will show you objectively, without letting negative thoughts or feelings tell you that you haven't made any progress. Are there still things you wish to address to reach your goals? And are you doing the things you hoped you would do if you began to feel better? Remember, reaching your goals will take time but with every step you take you are breaking that vicious circle.

If you feel better and ready to move on

If your mood has lifted and you feel that you are fully recovered then that is great! We are really pleased that you feel better. This is down to all the hard work that you have put in. You should be delighted. Please do ensure you now complete Section 4 (your relapse prevention toolkit) as this will help you continue to feel better.

In Section 4 we make a relapse prevention toolkit. This enables you to recognise your early warning signs and know what to do should you ever feel this way again. We hope that you don't, but we cannot predict if you will or not. People who have experienced depression may get it again in the future. The good news is that now you know things to do to regain control of your mood in the future. You have used BA successfully, and you have knowledge, skills and experience to put it into action again.

Antidepressant medication

If you are taking antidepressant medication, you should always consult your GP before you decide to reduce or stop taking it. Stopping an anti-depressant suddenly can cause serious problems. NICE guidance recommends you remain on your medication for several months after you feel better to keep your mood stable. Your GP will be able to advise when you can decrease or gradually stop it.

If you are feeling worse

> ### Key point: If at any time you feel much worse or have thoughts about ending your life
>
> If your mood has dropped really low and you have started to have thoughts about taking your own life, or have made plans about the way in which you would do this, then please seek further help. These thoughts can be really scary and distressing. Please tell someone how you are feeling and get the right support in place. These thoughts and feelings do not last forever and your mood will improve. Speak to your GP or another healthcare professional urgently.
>
> ### The Samaritans
>
> The Samaritans can be contacted via email, the phone or in person at one of their branches. Their volunteers are available 24 hours a day and will always pick up the phone. They can provide a listening ear and advice in times of crisis.

Phone: 08457 90 90 90

Post: Freepost RSRB-KKBY-CYJK, Chris, PO Box 90 90, Stirling, FK8 2SA

Email: Jo@samaritans.org

Website:http://www.samaritans.org/how-we-can-help-you/contact-us

You can also find more information about feeling suicidal and what you can do to get support on the NHS choices website here: http://www.nhs.uk/conditions/suicide/pages/introduction.aspx

Get Help straight away

If you are having thoughts about ending your life, have made a plan or intend to take any action towards harming yourself in any way, there are people you can talk to who want to help. Please ensure you:

- speak to a friend, family member or someone you trust. Confide in someone about how you are feeling

- contact the Samaritans 24-hour support service on 08457 90 90 90 or via the options given

above, or call the nearest A&E department and
tell the staff how you are feeling

- contact NHS

- make an urgent appointment to see your GP.

THE RELAPSE PREVENTION TOOLKIT

If you are reading this section, congratulations! This means that you have almost completed your CBT self-help and are hopefully feeling better. You have made progress towards the goals you set at the start. You have committed time and hard work in putting the techniques that you have learned into your daily life. You have successfully helped yourself to feel better.

The next – and final – step is to keep the progress going. To think about staying well and dealing with any difficulties that you may face in the future. We really encourage you to go this last step and work through this section.

For many people, reaching this point can be a really positive sign that things have improved. But also, it is understandably a time where you may be concerned about losing the progress that you have made. Or you may worry about having a relapse in the future.

Often people have concerns such as:

Will I cope by myself?

What do I do if I feel unwell again and where can I get help from?

Is there still work I need to do to stay well?

Will I slip back?

If a practitioner has been supporting you to work through this book, being discharged can also be concerning. You may wonder if you are ready or able to face going it alone without that support. Remember, it isn't the support from the practitioner alone that has helped you to feel better. It is the work you have done between sessions in your daily life that has achieved that. You have learned the skills to help yourself again. The support has helped you to motivate yourself. It has taught you the skills you need to put BA into action and to use those skills to lift your mood. Now you are feeling better this is something that you know that can do. Using this toolkit will help keep things on track.

When someone has been depressed and now feels better, it is understandable that they don't want to feel depressed again. For some people, however, this becomes a source of concern and worry. They try to avoid getting unwell again at all costs. This can mean that they look out for any signs or symptoms of feeling unwell again. They may mistake normal mood fluctuations for a sign that things are slipping back into a relapse of depression.

There are more helpful ways of managing your mood in the future and trying to prevent becoming depressed again. One is having a relapse prevention toolkit. In this section we want to help you put your own personalised helpful toolkit together.

You can think of this section as a toolkit to help you to:

- Know what the early warning signs were when you felt low or depressed before.

- Consider the things that may have kept you in that vicious circle, so you can spot them if they return. Any negative thoughts that you may have had. The things you did more or less of because of how you were feeling.

- Ensure you know how BA helped you to feel better and the steps that you took to make it work. Keeping your BA skills fresh using your wellbeing action plan means you will remember what to do should you need them again.

- Know where to get further help and support in the future should you need it.

Fluctuations in mood

Our mood can vary day to day when we are not depressed. We all have normal ups and downs. Before you felt depressed, your mood would have had ups and downs that lasted a few hours or days. And even now, you may have a lapse back into old ways of doing things. You might avoid things because of how you are feeling or thinking (working inside-out again rather than outside-in). The important thing is to recognise and ensure you understand the difference between a lapse and a relapse.

Being compassionate to yourself when you have a lapse is important. This means, don't expect your mood to be perfect every day. And don't worry that any symptoms you may have are a sign that you are back to square one.

Remember, you have the experience of managing your own mood successfully using BA. A lapse also does not mean that you have relapsed. There are times we may all act according to how we are thinking or feeling inside. For example, you have plans to see friends after work, but after a really busy day you're feeling tired and cancel. Every once in a while this is something we may all do. But it is when acting inside-out becomes a pattern you fall into regularly that you can get stuck in that vicious circle. It becomes a problem.

The best thing to do if you recognise that you have got into a pattern of acting inside-out again is to put your BA skills into action. Choose activities according to your plans, rather than how you may be thinking or feeling inside. Breaking this pattern before it takes hold will help again, just like it did before. You have the experience of having used it successfully and you can do so again.

Just like any new skill, BA requires regular practice. As part of your relapse prevention toolkit we will create a wellbeing action plan. Putting this into action reduces the likelihood of feeling low again. It also gives you confidence that you can spot any red flags that your mood is dropping and take action again.

What is the difference between a lapse and a relapse?

A **lapse** is a brief return to feeling down, or changes in what you do as a result. A lapse at times is normal. As long as we put into practice the BA techniques we have learned we can get back on track. A lapse can become a relapse if you allow it to take control of you. Worrying thoughts or seeing it as a sign of failure will contribute to this. The important thing is to see a lapse for what it is, just temporary. Don't let it make you give up doing things you need to do or make you dwell on failure. Acting against any off-putting thoughts, keeping doing things despite feeling like avoiding them, can prevent a lapse from becoming a relapse. Don't give up. Just keep doing the things in this guide that have helped you before.

A **relapse** is when negative thinking and avoidance behaviours creep back over a longer period. The vicious circle starts to spiral again, making you feel worse. But it is not a total setback. You have the skills and techniques that helped before to help you again, and you know it worked. The key thing is to notice early warning signs and to act your way out of it using the strategies that previously helped.

Unfortunately we cannot guarantee that you will never feel down again. It is normal for mood to fluctuate briefly for a few days or weeks at a time. Once you have been depressed before, then there is a chance that you could become unwell again in the future. However, the techniques and skills that you have learned will help you to act your way out of it should it happen again. This toolkit will help you to stay on track and to look out for your own early warning signs.

Early warning signs

Signs that it may be time to take action are if:

- Your lowered mood sticks around more days than not.

- You notice that you are getting back to ways of thinking and doing that did not help or back-fired before.

This is when it is time to put your BA skills back into action. Sometimes feeling unwell again may be triggered by a specific event but there may not be a particular trigger. Keeping to your wellbeing action plan for staying well means that if you do become unwell again you should spot it early. This will mean that feeling low again shouldn't be for as long or as intense as previously.

My early warning signs

Think about what symptoms you noticed when you began to feel unwell. We understand you may not want to dwell on these or think about them now you are feeling better. However, we really encourage you to spend some time identifying these symptoms: they are your early warning signs for the future.

The vicious circle diagram, below, will help you. In the diagram below write down what symptoms you noticed first:

- The **physical symptoms** you noticed first.

- The changes you noticed in **what you did** more or less of as a result.

- Any changes to the type of **thoughts** you had.

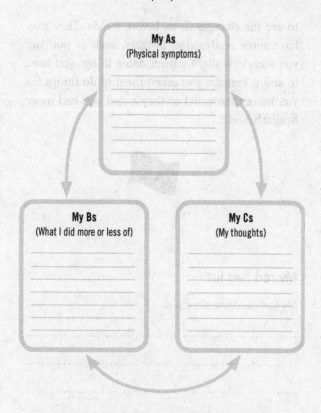

My As
(Physical symptoms)

My Bs
(What I did more or less of)

My Cs
(My thoughts)

When completing the vicious circle diagram you may want to turn back to the one you completed at the start of the book. Think about the time when you first felt unwell, before it got to the point where you decided to seek help. You may find it useful to speak to someone close and ask if there were any early signs they observed. Often other people start to see the changes in us before we do. They may have some really good insights, such as noticing you withdrew slightly from doing things you used to enjoy. Perhaps you asked them to do things for you more than usual or they noted you had more headaches, etc.

My red flag list

My early warning signs are:

....

....

....

....

....

....

....

If you, or someone you share your relapse plan with, spot signs that things on this red flag list are creeping back it is a good time to begin taking action. Use the BA techniques that helped you before, so that the vicious circle cannot take hold again. Remember to act according to your plans and not let off-putting negative thoughts or physical symptoms get in the way of your routine.

How things have improved since the start of treatment

Reflecting on your progress and how things have improved is an important part of relapse prevention. What things are you now doing that you were not doing when you felt unwell, for example? List here any changes you have noticed as signs of things improving for you:

....

....

....

....

....

....

....

....

....

....

....

....

List here the positive consequences of these improvements for you on different areas of your life.

Your work life

....

....

....

....

....

....

....

Things around the home

....

....

....

....

....

....

....

Your family life

....

....

....

....

....

....

....

Your friendships

....

....

....

....

....

....

Your social life

....

....

....

....

....

....

Re-rating my goals and targets

We asked you to set goals and targets at the start of this book. If you did, re-rate these again now using the form below and compare the progress you have made on each area.

Goal number 1: ....

Today's date...

At the start of the treatment I could do this:

| 0 | 1 | 2 | 3 | 4 | 5 | 6 |

I can do this now (circle a number):

| 0 | 1 | 2 | 3 | 4 | 5 | 6 |

Not at all   Occasionally   Often   Any time

Goal number 2: ....

Today's date...

At the start of the treatment I could do this:

| 0 | 1 | 2 | 3 | 4 | 5 | 6 |

I can do this now (circle a number):

| 0 | 1 | 2 | 3 | 4 | 5 | 6 |

Not at all   Occasionally   Often   Any time

Goal number 3: ....

Today's date...

At the start of the treatment I could do this:

| 0 | 1 | 2 | 3 | 4 | 5 | 6 |

I can do this now (circle a number):

| 0 | 1 | 2 | 3 | 4 | 5 | 6 |

Not at all   Occasionally   Often   Any time

Once you have measured your progress, take time to reflect upon how far you have come towards reaching those goals. Are there other things that have improved too?

....

....

....

What helped things to improve

What treatment techniques did you use that helped you move toward feeling better? These form a really important part of your toolkit for the future. List them here:

....

....

....

....

....

....

....

....

....

....

....

....

....

....

The wellbeing action plan

The other really helpful strategy for your toolkit is to develop is a wellbeing action plan. Set some time aside as your **wellbeing day** each month (or weekly if you can) to review the action plan and how you are feeling. This means you will hopefully pick up on early warning signs. It also means that you keep your BA skills fresh by revisiting the treatment that helped and how it works.

My wellbeing action plan

Keeping check of my mood
Review date:
How am I feeling this week/month (delete as applicable)?
Reading through my red flag list of early warning signs, have I had any that I am concerned about?

Have I got any signs of:

* Avoidance due to being anxious   yes/no

* Withdrawing or avoiding due to feeling down   yes/no

* Other old patterns of doing more of some   yes/no
  things that were unhelpful before?

Do I need to take any action now to keep feeling better?

If so, what helped before from my toolkit?

What do I need to do and when am I going to do it?

If things are going well, what is it that has been helping me?
Write in the vicious circle diagram the things I am doing in
each area to help keep things on track.

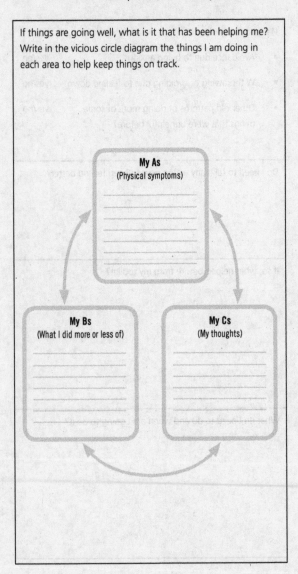

My As
(Physical symptoms)

My Bs
(What I did more or less of)

My Cs
(My thoughts)

Keeping my BA skills fresh

What are the key points of behavioural activation?

Even if you are feeling well, take a few moments to read through Section 3 again and the key points of how to use it and steps needed to carry it out. This is a great way to ensure you know what to do if you need the skills again.

Do I feel confident that I know how to use BA again if I needed to? What is the main way in which BA works?

Date of my next review day:

Put this on my calendar or phone so I will see it as a reminder.

Is there still anything you would like to work on?

Sometimes there are areas that you might still see change in. These may be goals that you set at the start of treatment that you would like to work on further. Or perhaps they are other things that you now would like to do.

If so what do you still want to do?

How will you do it?

When will you do it?

Are there any resources you need to do it?

What might get in the way of doing it and how can you overcome this?

Top tips from others

Below are some tips from other people who have worked through this book and professionals who have used BA.

Top tip 1	'The best way to prevent a lapse is to keep practising your CBT skills! If you are regularly practising, you will be in good shape to handle whatever situations you are faced with.'
Top tip 2	'Know your red flag early warning signs. Watch for times when you feel more stressed or when things happen in your life. I shared my list with my husband and he sometimes notices before me and reminds me to look through my toolkit.'
Top tip 3	'Use your wellbeing action plan even if you are feeling well. It really reminds me to look after me and to set aside time for myself.'
Top tip 4	'Put your wellbeing day on the calendar each month in a coloured pen, so you know it is your review time. Or add a note to your mobile, or leave a Post-it Note on the fridge!'
Top tip 5	'Be compassionate to yourself, we all have negative thoughts or times when we don't feel like doing things. Remember, it is doing the opposite that helps. When I notice I don't feel like doing something, like going to see a friend, I make sure I still go.'

Top tip 6	'Focus on the present moment. If you notice that you are having worrying thoughts, the best thing to do an activity that focuses your attention. It helps you to stop ruminating or worrying and making yourself feel worse.'
Top tip 7	'Think about small changes you can make that add up to big changes you may still want to do. Think of the big change as like the end destination you put in your Sat Nav. Even when it feels far off, there are roads you can take to get nearer to where you want to be. Just make sure you are still heading in the right direction.'
Top tip 8	'Reflect on how far you have come, too.'
Top tip 9	'Don't get too focused on reviewing your mood. Use your relapse prevention toolkit as often as you need to, with a regular wellbeing day that you stick to. Remember that your mood will fluctuate up and down at times – that is normal and OK!'

Getting further help if you need it

Sometimes if you have put into place all the options you can, managing your mood may still require additional support. Knowing where and how to get help is a good thing to have in your toolkit.

Where I can get more help

Think of a good friend, someone that you trust. Could you share this toolkit with them, so they can help you watch for your red flag early warning signs? They will then also know what you need to do to feel better. Write the name of someone you can identify as your toolkit supporter here:

....

Fill in the details of your GP here:

Surgery address:

....

....

....

Telephone number:

....

Also see the further resources at the end of the book for other useful organisations for support.

Congratulations!

You have come so far to reach this point, and we are delighted you stayed with the book and with us. Look what you have achieved as a result! Reflect on the progress you have made on the goals you set at the start. We know it may not have always been easy, and we cannot take any of the credit for you feeling better. That is all down to you – you alone are the reason that you are feeling better! We just provided the tools to help you to help yourself. It is down to the work you did using BA in your daily life.

The relapse prevention section will help you to keep feeling this way. It will make sure you know when to put the tools back into action, should you ever need to. The book is always here should you need it. Be proud of what you have done.

In the next section we return to Sarah and Bill to hear how they used CBT self-help to get well and stay well. You may have already read their stories earlier in the book. You may want to write your own story to add into it. This would be a lovely reminder of all the work you have done. Then, if you ever need to do more self-help, you can re-read it, knowing that you did it before and can do it again. Many people have found this a really helpful thing to do.

Others have written themselves a short letter celebrating how much better they feel. Then they ask a friend or relative to post it back to them in three months' time. It becomes a surprise reminder of what they have accomplished and can do again if they ever need to.

We have also provided a further resources section at the back. This has blank worksheets and details of useful information sources about depression and its treatment.

Good luck with your next steps and remember you have the skills to help yourself to feel better!

Marie and Paul

RECOVERY STORIES

Sarah's story

Sarah, the teacher who you met on page 35, experienced depression and used the CBT technique BA to feel better. Here is Sarah's recovery story. Her BA worksheets are here along with details of what she did. Although Sarah's situation may be different to your own, it will tell you more about using BA. From getting going to how Sarah overcame difficulties when planning and carrying it out.

"I was 54 when I was told by my GP that I had depression. He had asked me to complete a health questionnaire in the surgery. I was surprised to hear him say the word 'depressed' even though I knew things hadn't been right for a while. I had hoped he would tell me I was fine, and hurry me out of the door for his next appointment. Instead he referred me to the local therapy service. I was pleased that he had taken me seriously but was also devastated, to tell the truth. He signed me off work and I wondered how I had let things get so bad. I felt that I had let my students down, I wouldn't be there for them with exams coming up. If I am honest, I know that losing Mum and my osteoporosis diagnosis had hit me harder than I had realised. I had thrown myself into work as a way of distracting myself.

The head of the school I worked in retired, and a new head came in. She had her own view about which direction to take the school and it was very different to my own. I felt really undervalued and overlooked. She was also a micromanager; always asking questions and popping into my classes without warning. She seemed to dislike me from the start. I felt like I had to keep working harder and harder to prove myself. She would contact me in the evening and at weekends, and make critical remarks if I didn't respond straight away. I was exhausted all the time, but was hardly doing anything other than work. I felt like I had to work harder and harder just to keep my head above water.

Even before then, I had stopped doing things outside of work as much, like sports and seeing friends. It's true I was worried about becoming injured or fracturing something since being diagnosed with osteoporosis. But I think I also used it as an excuse to hide away as everything got too much. I just couldn't be bothered – everything seemed to take up so much energy. Then when my new boss came in, even work gave me no respite from how I was feeling. In fact it made it ten times worse.

My GP sent me to have an assessment by a practitioner named Emily at the therapy service. Emily said she worked using a CBT approach and told me how our thoughts, feelings and physical symptoms are linked. I had heard of CBT but didn't really know much about it before I went. She explained that when you are feeling depressed you avoid things that are difficult because of your symptoms. This helps in the short term, but it can backfire in the long term. It takes you away from your routine and social life, and things will start to pile up at home. It seemed such common sense when she said it like that. But when you are feeling down it's hard to see things as clearly when it is about yourself.

She gave me information to read later about a treatment called behavioural activation. She also made me an appointment for the following week, although I didn't think it could work for me at first. I was doing so much already with work that I didn't think I had the time or energy. Plus it looked so simple. How could just getting back to doing things help? And with my osteoporosis, would I really be able to, for a start? I took the booklet away anyway, but then left it in the bottom of my bag and carried on as usual.

I had a parents' evening on the Friday and stayed at work until it started. I went into my bag to get a pen and saw the booklet. It was partly curiosity and partly boredom, waiting for the parents to arrive, but I began to read through it. In it I read about someone who had used BA and thought to myself, 'What do I have to lose in giving it a go?' I knew deep down that it had been a long time since I had done anything I used to enjoy. Just work, and I didn't really enjoy that any more anyway. Things around the house had backed up too. I wasn't keeping the house clean or even changing the bed that often. It all just seemed too difficult. I knew I had been avoiding things as there were piles of unread mail and bills by the front door. BA seemed exactly what I needed to get things back on track.

While waiting for the first set of parents to arrive I filled out the first sheet. It was about what I had been avoiding since feeling down. Seeing it in black and white made me realise just how much my life had changed. I thought, 'If it could work for the person in the guide, just maybe it could work for me.'

I took my list back to my appointment with Emily. She didn't judge me. She just listened and then helped me to turn the list into a hierarchy – like a big ladder! We listed things that were difficult to get back to straight away and those that were less difficult. She explained I would start with things from the easier section and work up. I'd also keep a balance of the three types of activities across the week.

It all seemed difficult at first. It was hard to know what to put in the easier section. Emily helped me to be more specific than I had been on my first list. We broke things down so that they were more manageable, which really helped make things seem real. It was daunting. I wasn't sure I would be able to get going with it, but I really wanted to give it a try.

Emily said it was important to look at necessary tasks – those that have consequences if they are not done straight away. Those might need to be prioritised. I hadn't kept up with some of my bills

Activities I am avoiding as a result of how I feel		
Things that I do routinely (Washing-up, hoovering, grocery shopping, etc.)	Things that I used to enjoy or value (Hobbies, interests and sociable things, etc.)	Things that are necessary or there would be important consequences (Paying bills, taking prescribed medication, etc.)
Opening letters	Going to the gym	Paying bills: electric, car, gas, telephone and internet
Cleaning the house	Aerobics classes	Strength building exercises for my bones
Changing and making the bed	Seeing friends for coffee	
Supermarket shopping	Going out for meals with friends	
Loading the dishwasher	Keeping in touch with my family	
	Walking in the countryside	

as regularly as I normally would. Not because I couldn't, it just seemed so much effort to go and sort them. I hadn't even been opening the post. Together we discussed which bills they were and when they were likely to be due by. This helped me to see that some could wait. I had been fretting over them a lot without even opening them to see which was necessary first!

I had put strength exercises in as necessary, as I need to build bone strength. I had been advised to do some at home, using a booklet I had been given at the hospital. I hadn't done any, though, as it just reminded me about being unwell. I found it hard to get out of bed each day back then, so exercise was the last thing on my mind.

I explained to Emily that with osteoporosis there were some physical things I may not be able to do any more. I had stopped some exercise I actually liked in case it increased my risk of fracturing something. Emily said she had techniques that could be used within BA to help me to work around that. I had loved exercise at one point, but I hadn't been doing any since being diagnosed. Not even the exercises I was meant to do to strengthen my bones. I was terrified of breaking something and I just had no motivation since I'd started feeling down. I wasn't able to do the high-impact classes I used to enjoy, and so I had given up doing everything. There didn't seem any point.

When it came to putting exercise on the hierarchy, Emily asked me to think about what I valued about it. I hadn't really considered this before. I valued being strong and feeling exhilarated after a good work out. I had pushed myself hard as the classes I went to were about 45 minutes long without a break. I also valued the social aspect of it too. It was easy to get to know the people who went every week and I had made some good friends.

Emily helped me to think through things I could do at the gym that would reconnect me with those values. I had been given some information about exercise from a national charity when I first was diagnosed with osteoporosis. I could do strength-building exercises and ones that would help build bone density but not increase my risk of fractures. I hadn't really paid much attention to it as I had thrown myself into work. I thought the gym was in my past. The pictures in the booklet were of people much older than me. It made me feel frustrated and worn out, past my prime.

I was sceptical to say the least. I just imagined being sat at home with little dumbbells like the pictures in the booklet. She asked me to look online with her at what I might be able to do. She also liaised with my specialist nurse and GP. Together, we devised exercises for the hierarchy that would still give me that push and feeling of exhilaration. I knew I wasn't good at motivating myself much anyway, which is why I preferred using classes and having an instructor. Emily helped me realise that's what I needed – an instructor to keep me motivated. They would also push me while understanding what I could do. That was something I could work towards doing and break down into smaller tasks.

Emily asked me to finish off the hierarchy after that first session. I had to think of other ways to break down the more difficult tasks and to reconnect with things I valued.

We also made a plan to carry out two things from my easier section before I saw her again. We made a clear plan of what I was going to do and where.

My BA hierarchy	R, N or P
Most difficult	
Going for a long walk in the countryside	P
Cleaning out the garage	R
Buying a new car with the dealership when my current agreement comes to an end in two months' time	N
Doing a full monthly shop at the supermarket	R
Meeting Bridget and Sue for lunch	P
Medium difficulty	
Hoovering upstairs	R
Going for a 30-minute walk in the countryside	P
Meeting Bridget for lunch	P

Working out with a personal trainer	R
Doing strength exercises for my bone density	N
Sorting direct debits for the bills	N
Having a coffee with Sue	P
Less difficult	
Changing the bed	R
Going for a short walk in the first two fields	P
Ringing the gym about training sessions	N
Opening the post and putting it into piles	N

My BA planning diary: Week 1

AM	Monday	Tuesday	Wednesday	Thursday	Friday	Saturday	Sunday
What I am going to do?	Ring the gym and speak to them about personal training options.						Open the post that has built up and sort into piles of bills, junk and 'other'. Then add to my hierarchy the ones I need to deal with.
When I am doing it?	Ring from home in the morning at 10am when it opens.						At home in the dining room, alone, Sunday at 11am.
Where I am doing it?							
Am I planning to do it with anyone?							

PM	Monday	Tuesday	Wednesday	Thursday	Friday	Saturday	Sunday
What I am going to do?					Go for a short walk in the first two fields behind the house on Friday afternoon at 3pm.		
When I am doing it?							
Where I am doing it?							
Am I planning to do it with anyone?							

I made an effort to get up at the same time each day instead of staying in bed. I found this did help me to feel more in touch with things. That first week's BA tasks were not too difficult and it was motivating to have done them. Calling the gym where I still had my membership (paying monthly for not going!) was daunting, but I did it. They recommended a personal trainer called Tim who had worked with people with osteoporosis before. I made an appointment to see him the following week. I was nervous but pleased with myself for doing it.

My next appointment with Emily was over the phone and we were both pleased with how things had gone. We made a plan for the following week. I would do more tasks from my easier list and go to my gym appointment, which we added to the hierarchy. It was only to speak to Tim about exercises and options, so I felt OK with that. It didn't commit me to anything.

The following week's homework tasks started well. In fact things went so well I decided to add in a few more tasks to get things done. By the end of the week, though, I was exhausted and missed my appointment with Tim. I was really disappointed in myself. I nearly didn't bother going back to see Emily.

When I did see her next, I was close to giving up. Emily was really patient with me and took me back through the way in which BA works again. I had been doing things (or not!) because of how I was feeling. Doing too much that week had made me feel so tired that weekend, so I didn't make the appointment. I just lay in bed, rather than sticking to my plan, and then felt even worse. I knew I had got into the vicious circle again. Emily explained that often people who use BA can get into that pattern by doing too much too soon. That's why it is important to stick to the plan even if you feel like doing more.

It was nice to know I wasn't the only one who had done that. I guess I just wanted to feel better as quickly as possible and thought it would work straight away. Emily explained that the vicious circle had taken a while to build and it would take a while to improve – but it would. That really struck a chord. During that time, my head often felt fuzzy and I struggled to remember things, but that really ly stuck in my mind. If she had hope that I would improve, so should I. We made a new plan and the following week I stuck to it, including making a new appointment to see Tim and going this time. I kept going, remembering to keep to the plan, and I was really pleased that I did.

Over the following weeks of doing BA, things did start to improve. I was active again and began to feel better. I got into a routine and one day noticed that I was starting to enjoy things again. The feeling had been coming back but I really noticed it that day.

I am a big music fan and often had the radio on for background noise, even when I was depressed. On this particular day, one of my favourite songs came on and it made me sit up and take notice. I turned it up and sang along while I danced round my living room! It was such a great feeling. It wasn't always easy but I got there.

It was scary when Emily said I was ready to be discharged, but we made a plan together. I know what I need to do. I still have ups and downs, but I have come to acknowledge that that's OK. The downs will pass, if I don't let them control what I do. When I felt ready to go back to work, I did. They were supportive, but I applied for another post shortly afterwards at another school – and got the job! It was such a confidence boost and really showed me how far I have come. "

Bill's story

Bill, who you met on page 32, experienced depression and used BA to feel better alongside his antidepressant medication, fluoxetine. Here is Bill's story, which picks up during his treatment and will help you to see how he successfully used BA and made a recovery plan for remaining well.

" I was 65 years young when I had to leave work. I wasn't really ready to retire and to be honest hadn't prepared much for life after it. I didn't have anything to fill my time, and days seemed to pass by so slowly. Work had been such an important part of my social life. But when I retired I didn't feel like I should tag along with my old colleagues anymore. I was snappy and irritable with my wife, Pauline, and I was struggling to sleep. I had all these aches and pains and just didn't know what was wrong with me. I thought I should be able to snap out of it by myself, but weeks turned into months. It just kept getting worse.

Pauline had had enough and told me straight I had to get sorted. She came with me to see my GP. He gave me an antidepressant and suggested I get a self-help book that used behavioural activation. At first I wasn't sure this would work for me; I am not a big fan of taking tablets and don't read that much. But as Pauline said, 'If you had a headache you would take a tablet and do something about it, so why not give it a go?'

I took to BA really well and began to follow the steps in the book. It helped having Pauline to gently nudge me. It made sense to me and I liked the fact that it put me in control. Filling my ladder was initially difficult. Work had left a big gap which I had mainly filled with sitting around the house. It took time for me to think about the things I was avoiding doing, but there were plenty.

I really used to enjoy DIY and it was something that had built up. Pauline and I were keen to sell the house and downsize and there were lots of jobs waiting to be done. There were ones that I could do and others I needed to get someone in to do. I also wanted to fish and had been bought some rods as a leaving present. Pauline and I enjoyed going to antiques fairs in the past and we would have lunch on the way home. I even needed to just do a better job of looking after myself and showering each day. It sounds bad now, looking back, but at the time everything just seemed to sap my energy. Everything seemed to take so much effort that I often didn't bother. I wasn't helping around the house at all back then. With Pauline at work, I needed to pull my weight.

I think building things back in slowly and keeping a balance of things was what helped me most. It was really good when I went back to the GP a couple of weeks later. He said my scores had come down a little on the measure he did the first time I saw him. Although I didn't really feel better yet, it seemed like progress. It kept me going.

When I was depressed, I really struggled with being negative and going over things in my mind. Hours could pass and I wouldn't have moved from the chair, just going over and over things. It was helpful to read about rumination. I planned in activities to do at the times when I would often ruminate, which really helped. It got much better as the weeks went on. For me, this was the part of BA that really made the most difference as my negative thinking was genuinely problematic for me and had been so hard to snap out of. Before doing this, Pauline would get home from work and I would still be sat in the same chair, feeling miserable. It led to so much tension between us. Planning things in to break the pattern really worked and helped us to not be so irritable with each other.

It took several weeks to feel better, but it was such a great feeling when I did. I was keen to come off the medication but my GP advised I stay on it for a few months. This was to ensure things stayed on an even keel.

At first, I was really worried about getting down again and didn't want to end up feeling that way again. I must admit, when I began to feel better I didn't bother with the relapse prevention bit at first. The GP did ask me, and I said I would. But it was hard to want to do it when I was feeling OK again. Things were great compared to how they had been. I had done the decorating at home, ready to sell. I hadn't decorated our own house for years because I had been painting other people's day in, day out! Pauline and I had built back up our social lives together and with our friends from the village. All was going well, so why would I want to stop and think about my getting down again!?!

I had a day, though, where I just felt like staying in bed again. Some of those same negative thoughts crept back in. I thought, crikey, that's it – I am back to square one! I went to see my GP because I was so worried. He asked me if I was still taking the tablets (which I was). He also asked how I got on with the relapse prevention bit of the programme. I couldn't be dishonest and had to come clean that I hadn't got around to it.

He told me that normal mood fluctuates. The day I had was not a sign that things were going backwards, everyone has normal mood changes. He also told me about the difference between a lapse in mood and a relapse. He encouraged me to put a plan into place for using BA again should I need it. He said I should complete the early warning signs worksheet and follow the steps.

I talked it through with Pauline, as it recommended, and it was a really useful conversation. When I retired, she had noticed things were going off track long before I did. The first things she noticed were that I was becoming more irritable and having problems sleeping. That and the fact I stopped talking to her so much and seemed 'lost up in my head'. I noticed that I couldn't be bothered do to things any more. Everything seemed difficult, even sleeping.

Bill's red flag list

My early warning signs are:

Becoming more irritable

Having trouble getting off to sleep

Withdrawing from speaking to Pauline

Avoiding doing things because 'I can't be bothered'

Having lots of negative thoughts

Sitting ruminating over things

Waking up early and not being able to get back to sleep

Feeling really lethargic

Not being able to concentrate on TV or the paper

The plan helped me to plan having a review day. I think of this as a staying well day, rather than a day for dwelling on being unwell. It is taking a positive step to see how things are. Pauline sits with me too and we go through things together.

Going back through the steps of BA helps me to keep it fresh. I do notice that I am much more conscious of keeping things in balance and having a healthy routine. I have down days every now and again, but I make sure they don't affect what I do as a result.

Being depressed did come as a shock. It was hard work to get things on track. Although being depressed was a hard journey, now I can see that it also helped me to re-evaluate things. I feel I am now in a better place for having come through it, strange as that sounds. It taught me what is important. That we all need to look after ourselves and have plans in place to do things. The support of Pauline was invaluable and I think we are closer too. "

FURTHER RESOURCES

Extra worksheets

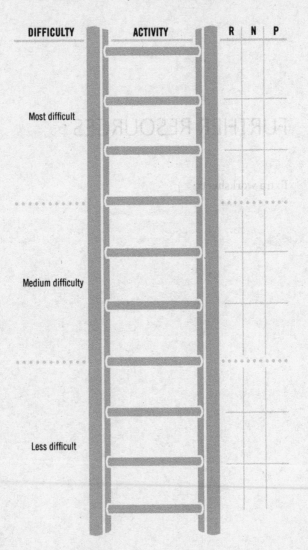

DIFFICULTY	ACTIVITY	R	N	P
Most difficult				
Medium difficulty				
Less difficult				

My BA planning diary: Week 1

AM	Monday	Tuesday	Wednesday	Thursday	Friday	Saturday	Sunday
What am I going to do?							
When am I doing it?							
Where am I doing it?							
Am I planning to do it with anyone?							

PM	Monday	Tuesday	Wednesday	Thursday	Friday	Saturday	Sunday
What am I going to do?							
When am I doing it?							
Where am I doing it?							
Am I planning to do it with anyone?							

My BA planning diary: Week 1

AM	Monday	Tuesday	Wednesday	Thursday	Friday	Saturday	Sunday
What am I going to do?							
When am I doing it?							
Where am I doing it?							
Am I planning to do it with anyone?							

PM	Monday	Tuesday	Wednesday	Thursday	Friday	Saturday	Sunday
What am I going to do?							
When am I doing it?							
Where am I doing it?							
Am I planning to do it with anyone?							

My BA planning diary: Week 1

AM	Monday	Tuesday	Wednesday	Thursday	Friday	Saturday	Sunday
What am I going to do?							
When am I doing it?							
Where am I doing it?							
Am I planning to do it with anyone?							

PM	Monday	Tuesday	Wednesday	Thursday	Friday	Saturday	Sunday
What am I going to do?							
When am I doing it?							
Where am I doing it?							
Am I planning to do it with anyone?							

My BA planning diary: Week 1

AM	Monday	Tuesday	Wednesday	Thursday	Friday	Saturday	Sunday
What am I going to do?							
When am I doing it?							
Where am I doing it?							
Am I planning to do it with anyone?							

PM	Monday	Tuesday	Wednesday	Thursday	Friday	Saturday	Sunday
What am I going to do?							
When am I doing it?							
Where am I doing it?							
Am I planning to do it with anyone?							

My BA planning diary: Week 1

AM	Monday	Tuesday	Wednesday	Thursday	Friday	Saturday	Sunday
What am I going to do?							
When am I doing it?							
Where am I doing it?							
Am I planning to do it with anyone?							

PM	Monday	Tuesday	Wednesday	Thursday	Friday	Saturday	Sunday
What am I going to do?							
When am I doing it?							
Where am I doing it?							
Am I planning to do it with anyone?							

My BA planning diary: Week 1

AM	Monday	Tuesday	Wednesday	Thursday	Friday	Saturday	Sunday
What am I going to do?							
When am I doing it?							
Where am I doing it?							
Am I planning to do it with anyone?							

PM	Monday	Tuesday	Wednesday	Thursday	Friday	Saturday	Sunday
What am I going to do?							
When am I doing it?							
Where am I doing it?							
Am I planning to do it with anyone?							

My BA planning diary: Week 1

AM	Monday	Tuesday	Wednesday	Thursday	Friday	Saturday	Sunday
What am I going to do?							
When am I doing it?							
Where am I doing it?							
Am I planning to do it with anyone?							

PM	Monday	Tuesday	Wednesday	Thursday	Friday	Saturday	Sunday
What am I going to do?							
When am I doing it?							
Where am I doing it?							
Am I planning to do it with anyone?							

My BA planning diary: Week 1

AM	Monday	Tuesday	Wednesday	Thursday	Friday	Saturday	Sunday
What am I going to do?							
When am I doing it?							
Where am I doing it?							
Am I planning to do it with anyone?							

PM	Monday	Tuesday	Wednesday	Thursday	Friday	Saturday	Sunday
What am I going to do?							
When am I doing it?							
Where am I doing it?							
Am I planning to do it with anyone?							

My BA planning diary: Week 1

AM	Monday	Tuesday	Wednesday	Thursday	Friday	Saturday	Sunday
What am I going to do?							
When am I doing it?							
Where am I doing it?							
Am I planning to do it with anyone?							

PM	Monday	Tuesday	Wednesday	Thursday	Friday	Saturday	Sunday
What am I going to do?							
When am I doing it?							
Where am I doing it?							
Am I planning to do it with anyone?							

My BA planning diary: Week 1

AM	Monday	Tuesday	Wednesday	Thursday	Friday	Saturday	Sunday
What am I going to do?							
When am I doing it?							
Where am I doing it?							
Am I planning to do it with anyone?							

PM	Monday	Tuesday	Wednesday	Thursday	Friday	Saturday	Sunday
What am I going to do?							
When am I doing it?							
Where am I doing it?							
Am I planning to do it with anyone?							

Reflection on my BA plan

Questions to ask myself about my week	My reflections
If I did my planned BA activities	How did it go? What did I notice before I did them? What did I notice afterwards? Did it impact on what I did for the rest of that day? How did it impact upon the next day, and how I felt and what I did as a result?

	What did I notice on the days where I had no planned activity in? Did I think or feel different as a result? What did I do on those days?
	What have I learned as a result of carrying out my BA activities?
	What does this mean for my plan for next week? What do I think I need to do as a result?
If I did not manage to carry out my plan	What stopped me from carrying out my plan?
	Was this an internal problem or an external one?

	How can I overcome this next time?
	What do I think I need to do next week as a result?
Were there any particular times that I noticed myself going over negative things in my mind (ruminating)?	If so, when was this?
	Did this happen when I was engaged in my planned activities or at other times during the week?
	What was I doing at that time?
	How did it impact on what I did and how I felt afterwards?

What does this teach me about my activity and my negative thoughts?

What may be helpful when planning activities next week and where I plan to fit them in as a result of this?

Reflection on my BA plan

Questions to ask myself about my week	My reflections
If I did my planned BA activities	How did it go?
	What did I notice before I did them?
	What did I notice afterwards?
	Did it impact on what I did for the rest of that day?
	How did it impact upon the next day, and how I felt and what I did as a result?

	What did I notice on the days where I had no planned activity in? Did I think or feel different as a result? What did I do on those days?
	What have I learned as a result of carrying out my BA activities?
	What does this mean for my plan for next week? What do I think I need to do as a result?
If I did not manage to carry out my plan	What stopped me from carrying out my plan?
	Was this an internal problem or an external one?

	How can I overcome this next time?
	What do I think I need to do next week as a result?
Were there any particular times that I noticed myself going over negative things in my mind (ruminating)?	If so, when was this?
	Did this happen when I was engaged in my planned activities or at other times during the week?
	What was I doing at that time?
	How did it impact on what I did and how I felt afterwards?

	What does this teach me about my activity and my negative thoughts?
	What may be helpful when planning activities next week and where I plan to fit them in as a result of this?

Reflection on my BA plan

Questions to ask myself about my week	My reflections
If I did my planned BA activities	How did it go?
	What did I notice before I did them?
	What did I notice afterwards?
	Did it impact on what I did for the rest of that day?
	How did it impact upon the next day, and how I felt and what I did as a result?

	What did I notice on the days where I had no planned activity in? Did I think or feel different as a result? What did I do on those days?
	What have I learned as a result of carrying out my BA activities?
	What does this mean for my plan for next week? What do I think I need to do as a result?
If I did not manage to carry out my plan	What stopped me from carrying out my plan?
	Was this an internal problem or an external one?

	How can I overcome this next time?
	What do I think I need to do next week as a result?
Were there any particular times that I noticed myself going over negative things in my mind (ruminating)?	If so, when was this?
	Did this happen when I was engaged in my planned activities or at other times during the week?
	What was I doing at that time?
	How did it impact on what I did and how I felt afterwards?

	What does this teach me about my activity and my negative thoughts?
	What may be helpful when planning activities next week and where I plan to fit them in as a result of this?

Reflection on my BA plan

Questions to ask myself about my week	My reflections
If I did my planned BA activities	How did it go?
	What did I notice before I did them?
	What did I notice afterwards?
	Did it impact on what I did for the rest of that day?
	How did it impact upon the next day, and how I felt and what I did as a result?

	What did I notice on the days where I had no planned activity in? Did I think or feel different as a result? What did I do on those days?
	What have I learned as a result of carrying out my BA activities?
	What does this mean for my plan for next week? What do I think I need to do as a result?
If I did not manage to carry out my plan	What stopped me from carrying out my plan?
	Was this an internal problem or an external one?

	How can I overcome this next time?
	What do I think I need to do next week as a result?
Were there any particular times that I noticed myself going over negative things in my mind (ruminating)?	If so, when was this?
	Did this happen when I was engaged in my planned activities or at other times during the week?
	What was I doing at that time?
	How did it impact on what I did and how I felt afterwards?

| | What does this teach me about my activity and my negative thoughts? |
| | What may be helpful when planning activities next week and where I plan to fit them in as a result of this? |

Reflection on my BA plan

Questions to ask myself about my week	My reflections
If I did my planned BA activities	How did it go?
	What did I notice before I did them?
	What did I notice afterwards?
	Did it impact on what I did for the rest of that day?
	How did it impact upon the next day, and how I felt and what I did as a result?

	What did I notice on the days where I had no planned activity in? Did I think or feel different as a result? What did I do on those days?
	What have I learned as a result of carrying out my BA activities?
	What does this mean for my plan for next week? What do I think I need to do as a result?
If I did not manage to carry out my plan	What stopped me from carrying out my plan?
	Was this an internal problem or an external one?

	How can I overcome this next time?
	What do I think I need to do next week as a result?
Were there any particular times that I noticed myself going over negative things in my mind (ruminating)?	If so, when was this?
	Did this happen when I was engaged in my planned activities or at other times during the week?
	What was I doing at that time?
	How did it impact on what I did and how I felt afterwards?

What does this teach me about my activity and my negative thoughts?

What may be helpful when planning activities next week and where I plan to fit them in as a result of this?

Reflection on my BA plan

Questions to ask myself about my week	My reflections
If I did my planned BA activities	How did it go?
	What did I notice before I did them?
	What did I notice afterwards?
	Did it impact on what I did for the rest of that day?
	How did it impact upon the next day, and how I felt and what I did as a result?

	What did I notice on the days where I had no planned activity in? Did I think or feel different as a result? What did I do on those days?
	What have I learned as a result of carrying out my BA activities?
	What does this mean for my plan for next week? What do I think I need to do as a result?
If I did not manage to carry out my plan	What stopped me from carrying out my plan?
	Was this an internal problem or an external one?

	How can I overcome this next time?
	What do I think I need to do next week as a result?
Were there any particular times that I noticed myself going over negative things in my mind (ruminating)?	If so, when was this?
	Did this happen when I was engaged in my planned activities or at other times during the week?
	What was I doing at that time?
	How did it impact on what I did and how I felt afterwards?

	What does this teach me about my activity and my negative thoughts?
	What may be helpful when planning activities next week and where I plan to fit them in as a result of this?

Reflection on my BA plan

Questions to ask myself about my week	My reflections
If I did my planned BA activities	How did it go?
	What did I notice before I did them?
	What did I notice afterwards?
	Did it impact on what I did for the rest of that day?
	How did it impact upon the next day, and how I felt and what I did as a result?

	What did I notice on the days where I had no planned activity in? Did I think or feel different as a result? What did I do on those days?
	What have I learned as a result of carrying out my BA activities?
	What does this mean for my plan for next week? What do I think I need to do as a result?
If I did not manage to carry out my plan	What stopped me from carrying out my plan?
	Was this an internal problem or an external one?

	How can I overcome this next time?
	What do I think I need to do next week as a result?
Were there any particular times that I noticed myself going over negative things in my mind (ruminating)?	If so, when was this?
	Did this happen when I was engaged in my planned activities or at other times during the week?
	What was I doing at that time?
	How did it impact on what I did and how I felt afterwards?

What does this teach me about my activity and my negative thoughts?

What may be helpful when planning activities next week and where I plan to fit them in as a result of this?

Reflection on my BA plan

Questions to ask myself about my week	My reflections
If I did my planned BA activities	How did it go?
	What did I notice before I did them?
	What did I notice afterwards?
	Did it impact on what I did for the rest of that day?
	How did it impact upon the next day, and how I felt and what I did as a result?

	What did I notice on the days where I had no planned activity in? Did I think or feel different as a result? What did I do on those days?
	What have I learned as a result of carrying out my BA activities?
	What does this mean for my plan for next week? What do I think I need to do as a result?
If I did not manage to carry out my plan	What stopped me from carrying out my plan?
	Was this an internal problem or an external one?

	How can I overcome this next time?
	What do I think I need to do next week as a result?
Were there any particular times that I noticed myself going over negative things in my mind (ruminating)?	If so, when was this?
	Did this happen when I was engaged in my planned activities or at other times during the week?
	What was I doing at that time?
	How did it impact on what I did and how I felt afterwards?

| | What does this teach me about my activity and my negative thoughts? |
| | What may be helpful when planning activities next week and where I plan to fit them in as a result of this? |

Reflection on my BA plan

Questions to ask myself about my week	My reflections
If I did my planned BA activities	How did it go? What did I notice before I did them?
	What did I notice afterwards? Did it impact on what I did for the rest of that day? How did it impact upon the next day, and how I felt and what I did as a result?

	What did I notice on the days where I had no planned activity in? Did I think or feel different as a result? What did I do on those days?
	What have I learned as a result of carrying out my BA activities?
	What does this mean for my plan for next week? What do I think I need to do as a result?
If I did not manage to carry out my plan	What stopped me from carrying out my plan?
	Was this an internal problem or an external one?

	How can I overcome this next time?
	What do I think I need to do next week as a result?
Were there any particular times that I noticed myself going over negative things in my mind (ruminating)?	If so, when was this?
	Did this happen when I was engaged in my planned activities or at other times during the week?
	What was I doing at that time?
	How did it impact on what I did and how I felt afterwards?

What does this teach me about my activity and my negative thoughts?

What may be helpful when planning activities next week and where I plan to fit them in as a result of this?

Reflection on my BA plan

Questions to ask myself about my week	My reflections
If I did my planned BA activities	How did it go?
	What did I notice before I did them?
	What did I notice afterwards?
	Did it impact on what I did for the rest of that day?
	How did it impact upon the next day, and how I felt and what I did as a result?

	What did I notice on the days where I had no planned activity in? Did I think or feel different as a result? What did I do on those days?
	What have I learned as a result of carrying out my BA activities?
	What does this mean for my plan for next week? What do I think I need to do as a result?
If I did not manage to carry out my plan	What stopped me from carrying out my plan?
	Was this an internal problem or an external one?

	How can I overcome this next time?
	What do I think I need to do next week as a result?
Were there any particular times that I noticed myself going over negative things in my mind (ruminating)?	If so, when was this?
	Did this happen when I was engaged in my planned activities or at other times during the week?
	What was I doing at that time?
	How did it impact on what I did and how I felt afterwards?

| | What does this teach me about my activity and my negative thoughts? |
| | What may be helpful when planning activities next week and where I plan to fit them in as a result of this? |

Further information

The NHS Choices website has excellent resources to find out more about depression. This includes a video that outlines the symptoms of depression, early warning signs and what can be done about it. You can watch it on the NHS Choices website with the following link: http://www.nhs.uk/Conditions/Depression/Pages/Introduction.aspx

The Charity MIND have also created excellent resources about what depression is. This includes a short film of people who have had depression sharing their experiences and their own journeys using

CBT treatments: http://www.mind.org.uk/informa tion-support/types-of-mental-health-problems/ depression

You can find more information about medications for depression on the NHS Choices website here: http://www.nhs.uk/conditions/ssris-(selective-sero tonin-reuptake-inhibitors)/Pages/Introduction. aspx

Support

Talk to your GP, who has access to a range of services that deliver support for CBT self-help.

In England, the IAPT (Improving Access to Psychological Therapies) provides support and counselling for individuals. Find out here where each service is and how to contact them: http:// www.iapt.nhs.uk/services/.

If you are feeling suicidal

If you are feeling suicidal and having thoughts of ending your life, this can be really scary and distressing. Please tell someone how you are feeling and get the right support in place. These thoughts and feelings do not last forever and your mood will improve. Suicide is not the answer. Please remember that these thoughts are just that, thoughts. They can just pop into your mind when you are feeling down and low, so can take you by surprise. Speak to your GP or another healthcare professional urgently.

The Samaritans can be contacted via email, the phone or in person at one of their branches. Their volunteers are available 24 hours a day and will always pick up the phone. They can provide a listening ear and advice in times of crisis.

Phone: 08457 90 90 90

Post: Freepost RSRB-KKBY-CYJK, Chris, PO Box 90 90, Stirling, FK8 2SA

Email: Jo@samaritans.org

Website: http://www.samaritans.org/how-we-can-help-you/contact-us

You can also find more information about feeling suicidal and what you can do to get support on the NHS choices website here: http://www.nhs.uk/conditions/suicide/pages/introduction.aspx

DEDICATIONS AND ACKNOWLEDGEMENTS

Marie:

Firstly, I would like to dedicate this book to all the people with depression I have had the privilege to work with over the years. They have inspired and taught me so much through their resilience and strength. It is also dedicated to the practitioners that I have trained and supervised through IAPT who work so hard to make an invaluable difference to so many people's lives. Also to those who have given me ideas and feedback for this book, as well demonstrating their generosity in being willing to share their hints and tips with others. Lastly, it cannot be forgotten that it is only because of the determination and dedication of Professor David Richards and his seminal work on depression, BA and low-intensity CBT training that we are now in the fortunate position to have PWPs supporting people with depression across England, Australia and beyond.

I have written this book in loving memory of my mother, Bridget Mary Chellingsworth, 1939–2008. *'In the light that shines through your window, I'll be everywhere'*

Paul:

During the writing of this book I was taken seriously ill, nearly dying on two occasions. Firstly, I would like to dedicate this book to my wife Paula, children Oliver, Ellis and Amélie, and family and friends, for all their love, never giving up hope and for their personal resilience, keeping everything going during this difficult time for us all. Furthermore I would like to dedicate this book to the surgical, medical and nursing staff at Pencarrow and Clearbrook wards in Derriford Hospital, Plymouth, and Bolham and Creedy wards, Mardon Neuro-Rehabilitation Centre at the Royal Devon & Exeter hospital, and the Exeter and Honiton dialysis units. My experience on the other side of the fence, as a patient, has really confirmed to me what a truly great asset the NHS and all those who work within it are, and how we should fight to protect it at all costs.

Acknowledgements

In writing this book we acknowledge the seminal work of Professor David Richards, Dave Ekers and

Karina Lovell in bringing behavioural activation to the attention of the UK through their research and clinical development of its effectiveness. We are also indebted to the editorial and publishing team who have been patient with us in getting the book finished and into print through illness and adversity.

INDEX

How to Beat Worry and
Generalised Anxiety One Step at a Time

Using evidence-based low-intensity CBT

Marie Chellingsworth and Paul Farrand

ISBN: 978-1-47210-885-2 (paperback)

ISBN: 978-1-47211-344-3 (ebook)

Price: £7.99

Publication date: February 2016

This book is the perfect resource for helping you to beat worry or Generalised Anxiety Disorder, either by yourself or in conjunction with the support of an IAPT service. It is written in a friendly, engaging (and jargon-free!) style and encourages interactive reading through tables, illustrations and worksheets. Real-life case studies illustrate the use of each intervention and demonstrate how you can work through your anxiety. You will learn effective techniques for managing your worry by keeping a Worry Diary; scheduling a daily Worry Time; using a Practical Problem Solving approach; and releasing tension through Progressive Muscle Relaxation.

How to Beat Panic Disorder
One Step at a Time

Using evidence-based low-intensity CBT

Paul Farrand and Marie Chellingsworth

ISBN: 978-1-47210-884-5 (paperback)

ISBN: 978-1-47211-343-6 (ebook)

Price: £7.99

Publication date: May 2016

This book is the perfect resource for helping you to beat Panic Disorder, either by yourself or in conjunction with the support of an IAPT service. It is written in a friendly, engaging (and jargon-free!) style and encourages interactive reading through tables, illustrations and worksheets. Real-life case studies illustrate the use of each intervention and demonstrate how you can work through your moments of panic. You will learn effective techniques from Cognitive Behavioural Therapy that have been shown to work for people with panic disorder.

How to Beat Panic Disorder
One Step at a Time

Using evidence-based low-intensity CBT

Paul Farrand and Marie Chellingsworth

ISBN 978-1-47210-884-5 (paperback)

ISBN 978-1-47210-913-2 (ebook)

Price £9.99

Publication date: June 2016

This book is one part of 'The resource for helping you to beat Panic Disorder, by either doing it yourself or in combination with the support of an IAPT service. It is written in a friendly, engaging and supportive way to overcome common difficulties, pulling through tasks, illustrations and worksheets that help the reader to work through your thoughts of panic. You will learn effective techniques to recognise behaviours. These ideas have been shown to work for people with anxiety.